In
Nietzsche's
Footsteps

Jonathan R. Cohen

8th House Publishing
Montreal, Canada

Copyright © 8th House Publishing 2018
First Edition

Published worldwide by 8th House Publishing.
Front Cover Design by 8th House Publishing

Designed by 8th House Publishing.
www.8thHousePublishing.com

Set in Garamond, Delicious Heavy, Raleway and Caslon.

LIBRARY AND ARCHIVES CANADA CATALOGUING IN PUBLICATION

Cohen, Jonathan, 1958-, author
    In Nietzsche's footsteps / Jonathan R. Cohen.

Includes bibliographical references and index.
ISBN 978-1-926716-48-0 (softcover)

    1. Nietzsche, Friedrich Wilhelm, 1844-1900--Homes and haunts.
2. Nietzsche, Friedrich Wilhelm, 1844-1900. 3. Individualism. I. Title.

B3316.C63 2018   193   C2018-904911-1

IN
NIETZSCHE'S
FOOTSTEPS

Jonathan R. Cohen

8TH HOUSE PUBLISHING

༠Acknowledgments

THE FIRST person to thank is Paul Gies and he has no idea why. When I was Director of General Education at my university and felt a need to make my campus-wide emails breezy and charming to develop support for the projects I was trying to promote, Paul, who is a mathematician and a notoriously sharp-cursored emailer, responded to one of them by saying, "Jonathan! (that's how he addresses his emails—first name plus exclamation point) That last e-mail sounded so much like *you*!" And this made me realize that without really trying to, I had developed a voice, and this gave me the confidence to try it out on a non-scholarly piece and now, dear reader, you hold it in your hands. So thanks, Paul.

The second person to thank is Michael Burke and he too has no idea why. Michael used to teach at my university and his book, which concerns a white-water adventure undertaken during the last months of his wife's pregnancy, wasn't published until his daughter graduated from high school. This has given me the confidence to keep going despite taking so long on my own book that my own children have grown far beyond the forms in which they are depicted here, having outgrown (among other things) the way their size order matched their age order. Since walking in Nietzsche's footsteps, we have gone on many other trips as a family, all of the children have graduated from high school and two from college. Three presidential elections have come and gone, computer chips have evolved to a fraction of their former size, untold empires have risen and fallen, thousands of species have gone extinct while a few new ones have evolved, *et cetera,* and yet here I am still tapping away hopefully. So thanks, Michael.

The third thanks goes to the University of Maine at Farmington for funding a sabbatical during which I was able to get some sort of grasp on my material and write a couple drafts of the book.

Fourth comes thanks to all those who read this piece in draft: Linda Britt, Kristen Case, Gretchen Legler and especially Matthew Freytag who, having lived as both a philosophical nomad and as a family man, knew both sides of this book's "equation" and whose comments from both perspectives were immeasurably helpful. Thanks for the final round of editing goes to Emery Moreira, Annah-Lauren Bloom and Victoria Cohen.

Fifth, finally, and most of all—thanks to my family. I will go on to assert a few pages from now that I could have lived Nietzsche's way, a solitary wanderer alone with his notebook; my family might not believe it, but it's really true. And so, I have to thank them for providing me the space, opportunity and encouragement to cook, ski, appreciate new music, see movies I wouldn't have otherwise, hear concerts I wouldn't have attended, do countless other things I couldn't have imagined doing previously, and, of course, play hearts—in short, for constraining me to live. Nietzsche writes a lot about "the needs of life," but the one he never mentions is family. His philosophy is the lesser for it, and mine the better for it (though his is still better, of course). Anyway—thanks, guys.

DEDICATION

EVERY FAMILY has their special way of approaching travel. Our way is that we never, ever check baggage.

A series of bad experiences convinced us of this: It's not that airlines do a bad job with checked luggage; it's that they simply *do not care*.

Once, one of our checked bags contained a passport. Once, my checked bag contained the paper I was supposed to read the next day at a conference.

Never again.

Now we travel light everywhere, no matter the distance, no matter the occasion, no matter the time span. It's just safer to do laundry. As a result, our children, pretty much from the time they could walk, have had their own rollaboards. Go online and check them out: Luggage companies make these really cute, toddler-sized rollaboards and every little bit helps.

And so when we go through airports, we form a line of six rollaboarders of various heights, pulling six rollaboards of various sizes and colors, and we troop duckling-style through the concourses and walkways, up and down the escalators, round and about the terminals.

One time years ago, to keep up morale and to validate their efforts—and because they looked so darn cute all in a line, pulling their rollaboards—my wife dubbed our kids "The Professional Travelers."

It is to them that this book is dedicated.

Alas, where shall I climb now with my longing? From all mountains I look out for fatherlands and motherlands. But home I found nowhere; a fugitive am I in all cities and a departure at all gates. Strange and a mockery to me are the men of today to whom my heart recently drew me; and I am driven out of fatherlands and motherlands. Thus I now love only my children's *land, yet undiscovered, in the farthest sea: for this I bid my sails search and search.*[1]

---

1   Z II.14

In
NIETZSCHE'S
FOOTSTEPS

SOURCES FOR QUOTATIONS

Key to citations:

A = *The Antichrist*, trans. Kaufmann
BT = *The Birth of Tragedy*, trans. Kaufmann
CW = *The Case of Wagner*, trans. Kaufmann
BGE = *Beyond Good and Evil*, trans. Kaufmann
EH = *Ecce Homo*, trans. Kaufmann
GM = *On the Genealogy of Morals*, trans. Kaufmann
GS = *The Gay Science*, trans. Kaufmann
HAH = *Human, All-too-Human*, trans. Hollingdale
NCW = *Nietzsche Contra Wagner*, trans. Kaufmann
T = *Twilight of the Idols*, trans. Kaufmann
UM = *Untimely Meditations*, trans. Hollingdale
Z = *Thus Spoke Zarathustra*, trans. Kaufmann

Allison = *The New Nietzsche*, David Allison, Dell, 1977
Chamberlain = *Nietzsche in Turin*, Picador USA, 1996
Hayman = *Nietzsche: A Critical Life*, Penguin Books, 1982
Kaufmann = *Nietzsche*, Princeton Univ Press, 4th edition, 1975
Kierkegaard = *Concluding Unscientific Postscript*, transl. Hong, Howard & Hong, Edna, Princeton University Press, rev ed. 2013
Krell & Bates = *The Good European*, Univ of Chicago Press, 1997
Middleton = *Selected Letters of Friedrich Nietzsche*, originally published University of Chicago Press, 1969, reprinted by Hackett Publishing Company, 1996
The Portable Nietzsche, ed. Kaufmann, The Viking Press, 1954, reprinted by Penguin Books, 1976

Nietzsche's works are cited by work and section number, Middleton by letter number, and the others by page number.

C ONTENTS

ACKNOWLEDGMENTS   v
DEDICATION   vii
Prologue - Deciding Where to Go   5
Nationalism to Nomadism   11
On Our Way   23
Amor Fati and *Ressentiment* in Bavaria   35
Perspectivism in Nice   41
Watering the Soul in the Riviera   54
Living Nietzschean in Old Nice   63
The Eternal Recurrence of Èzé   73
The Nietzschean Hike   90
Nice *Moderne:*   104
Nietzsche & the Artist   104
Ascent: Nice to Turin   115
Shabbat – *chiuso per restauro*   129
Morality & Flogging Horses   137
Nobility & the Last Man   148
Will to Power in the Molé Tower   158
Ascent to Sils-Maria   185
Living Dangerously   192
Perspectivism & the View from Above   207
Nietzsche's Dream *Haus*   215
My Children's Land   225
Epilogue   230

Index   234

Prologue - Deciding Where to Go

IN 2008 THE PROFESSIONAL Travelers were old enough—Sam seventeen, Rosie fifteen, Eli twelve, and Miriam ten—to appreciate and remember a trip to Europe. But Europe's a big place—where exactly would we go? Vicky and I told the kids to poke around online, and the two of us did too, in between our other responsibilities. We got travel books from the library. I looked again at my old copy of *Let's Go: Europe*. It became the main topic of our dinnertime conversation throughout the winter, with everyone pushing a different destination.

Finally, Vicky, recognizing that I would be turning fifty in the coming summer, asked me if there was anywhere I had always wanted to go. "Well," I said, "I've always been curious to see Turin. It was Nietzsche's favorite city—the place he lived for the final months of his conscious life—and in his letters he makes it sound really marvelous."

So we started looking at Turin (Torino in Italian, but I'll stick mostly with Turin since that's the name Nietzsche and his biographers all use). It's not a place American tourists tend to visit, but it has some nice attractions. In addition, Turin happens to be the place where Europeans first figured out what to do with the chocolate that the conquistadors had brought back from the New World. The key had been to add sugar, thus creating what to my family constitutes a food group all its own. We started to consider Turin and possibly combining it with Venice and other northern Italian towns.

"Although you know," I added a couple days later, "I've also always wanted to see Sils-Maria, in Switzerland. It's a small town near St. Moritz. It's where Nietzsche spent his summers. His boarding house has been preserved as a sort of small museum for him. There's also a plaque at the spot where he thought of the Eternal Recurrence. I've always wanted to make a pilgrimage there."

A few days later I opened *The Good European*. This is a book by Nietzsche scholar David Farrell Krell and photographer Donald L. Bates which offers photographs of many of the places Nietzsche lived and visited, along with passages from Nietzsche's writings and letters which either mention these places directly or, just as powerfully, read as if inspired by them.

Leafing through this remarkable book—without which, I freely admit, the present one could not have been written—I came upon a letter I had seen before in biographies of Nietzsche but hadn't fully appreciated. Nietzsche wrote it in 1888 shortly after establishing residence at what fast became his favorite city:

> I have discovered *Turin*... Turin is not a well-known city, is it? The educated German travels right on by it. Granted my hardness of heart in the face of everything that education commends, I have established Turin as my *third* residence, with Sils-Maria as the first and Nice as the second. Four months at each place: in the case of Turin it is two months in the spring and two in the fall....[2]

2   Letter to Reinhart von Seydlitz, May 13, 1888, in Krell & Bates 224

I read Vicky the letter to explain Nietzsche's love of Turin, but then was struck by the other places mentioned. Sils-Maria I had long thought of, but not Nice. I recalled that Nietzsche signed some of his prefaces from the 1880's as having been written in Nizza, which is the Italian for Nice, but that was pretty much all I knew about it. We looked at a map and saw that Nice, Turin and Sils-Maria form a line running southwest to northeast. Together they offer three different geographical zones, the Riviera, the Piedmont and the Alps, as well as five different languages—French, Italian, German, Niçard, which we eventually learned is a Provençal dialect spoken only in Nice, and Romansh, a unique blend of Romance and Germanic linguistic sources spoken in the Engadine region of Switzerland where Sils-Maria is located. Touring these three places, we would see beaches and mountains, modern art galleries and Roman ruins, urban piazzas and Alpine scenery.

Nice then, completed the perfect European sampler set. And with that, we had our itinerary: Nice, Turin, Sils-Maria, about five days in each. Sam investigated train travel; Rosie looked for craft markets; Eli scouted parks and hikes; and Miriam reviewed museums and restaurants. We acquired guidebooks, maps, and phrasebooks, and began packing the rollaboards.

IN my mind, I gave the trip a formal title, "In Nietzsche's Footsteps," which I thought appropriate in two ways—not only would we be following the path of Nietzsche's peregrinations from residence to residence, we would also be walking on many of the actual streets and pathways that he is known to have walked. Nietzsche walked daily and vigorously, sometimes for as long as seven or eight hours at a stretch, carrying a pocket notebook. Many of his ideas came to him at these times and many passages in his writings were begun on foot. In his autobiography, *Ecce Homo* (written in Turin), he shares his personal code for day-to-day living, of which this is part:

> *Sit* as little as possible; give no credence to any thought that was not born outdoors while one moved about freely—in which the muscles are not celebrating a feast, too.... The sedentary life... is the real sin against the holy spirit.[3]

I take him to mean this both physiologically (an oxygenated mind works better, we would say now) and experientially— one is out in the world, engaged with it as opposed to being cloistered in some office or library immured from real life.

"In Nietzsche's Footsteps" seemed to me at the same time a fitting title for a writing project in which I would discuss Nietzsche's life and writings. But it took no time at all for the irony to hit. I might be following physically in Nietzsche's footsteps, but in my life plan I haven't followed him at all. I chose to be a husband, a family man, a job-holder, while Nietzsche chose a solitary life. After his father and brother died young, Nietzsche fled from his mother and sister. He resigned his academic post, officially because of illness but also because of mutual disenchantment. He was rejected by the only woman he ever loved, as well as various others to whom he made brief and mutually embarrassing proposals. He broke with friend after friend. He lived as a wanderer, moving from boarding house to boarding house, changing his residence several times a year and sometimes several times

---

3   EH clever.1

a month. He broke down at the age of forty-four from too much strain, too much work and too much solitude.[4] He didn't reach fifty, at least not with any consciousness left to him. He didn't have a wife and he didn't have children. Unlike me, he broke with the religion of his upbringing.

In fact, Nietzsche and I are so different it's a wonder I'm allowed to teach and write about him at all. How could I possibly understand someone so dissimilar? How can I claim to be a devotee of his work when I don't seem to have followed his example at all? How can I say he taught me things when I don't seem to have learned anything from him? I tell people he's a great philosopher in part because he brings philosophy to earth and provides insight as to how to live, yet I don't seem to be living by his precepts at all.

This paradox might be a wholly personal matter if not for the fact that Western culture itself follows in Nietzsche's footsteps in a sense. Anyone who studies Nietzsche can easily see his philosophy at work in the world around us, in the decline of religion, of belief in absolute truth, and of nationalism,[5] and conversely in the ascendance of scientific naturalism, perspectivism, individualism, and European cultural cosmopolitanism. And so people who participate in these cultural changes—which is pretty much all of us, or will be, once you account for globalization—are, whether we know it or not, following in Nietzsche's footsteps as well.

But here's the issue—*should* we follow in Nietzsche's

---

4   And all of this probably piled on top of an underlying medical condition. Until fairly recently, Nietzsche's biographers usually attributed the breakdown to syphilis, although I must say this never struck me as especially plausible in light of the paucity of Nietzsche's sexual activity. The most recent research changes the preferred diagnosis to slowly growing right-sided retro-orbital meningioma. See Leonard Sax, "What was the Cause of Nietzsche's Dementia?" *Journal of Medical Biography* 2003; 11: 47–54.
5   As this book goes to press, nationalism appears to be on the upswing again, but I would argue that this is a backlash against an undeniable movement towards increased integration across national lines.

footsteps? We can examine this question in the context of a lived life with Nietzsche as example. "I profit from a philosopher only insofar as he can be an example,"[6] said Nietzsche, writing about Schopenhauer, but meaning it for all philosophers. What example does Nietzsche set in both his life and his thought? *Can* he be followed and if so, would it be wise to do so?

Nationalism to Nomadism

SOME INFORMATION is needed before we can understand why we're traveling this itinerary. How did it come to be that this German philosopher lived half of his life outside of Germany? How did it come to be that this brilliant scholar had no fixed home? Why is it that walking in Nietzsche's footsteps requires travel to France, Italy, and Switzerland?

Nietzsche was born October 15, 1844, in Röcken, a small town in Saxony, a province of Prussia. His father, a Lutheran minister, died when Nietzsche was just five years old. (Those who wish to see some significance in this for a man who later proclaimed that God is dead are hereby not discouraged from doing so.) We now suspect that the cause of his father's death was a bad fall and resulting concussion, but Nietzsche himself believed that the cause of death was "softening of the brain." This belief, and the accompanying superstition that the condition was hereditary, hung over Nietzsche his entire life. On the one hand, he expected to meet the same fate at the same age (thirty-six), so that when he had a stretch of bad health in 1880, he thought it might be his end. Surviving it, he felt he had been granted an unexpected windfall of life, and the simple thrill of being alive that marks his writings through the rest of the 1880's is unmistakable.

Nietzsche was raised by his mother, a pious, well-meaning, but (in her son's eyes, at least) mostly ineffectual person. He had a younger brother, but only briefly—the brother died at age two, about a year after the death of his father. The rest of the household consisted of a younger sister, Elisabeth, two maiden aunts and his grandmother. (Those who wish to see some significance in this all-female household for Nietzsche's later misogyny are hereby not discouraged from doing that either.)

Nietzsche was a studious, bookish child. He and his friends, at age ten, formed a little intellectual society which required that they prepare and give lectures to each other on various scholarly topics. At least, Nietzsche gave some lectures—it's not clear whether his friends were able to give any also, or to keep up with him when he was speaking. He went to prestigious boarding schools and was a star student. He studied theology and classics at university. The former interest dropped away early on, along with his faith, angering his mother. He was so good at the latter, however, that in 1868 at the tender age of twenty-four, even before finishing his doctorate, he was awarded the prestigious chair of classics at the University of Basel. In part this was a credit to the renown of his teacher, Jakob Ritschl, who scored similar appointments for several of his students. Nevertheless, to this day Nietzsche remains one of the youngest tenured professors ever, anywhere in the world.

His academic career did not go particularly well, however. The problem was not a too-brief apprenticeship. Rather, Nietzsche's personality—ever eager to overturn things and not much given to team-playing—was not well-suited for academia. For example, Nietzsche's first published work, *The Birth of Tragedy,* defied all scholarly propriety. It made no reference to previous scholarship, giving instead a very intuitive analysis of Greek tragedy, only to close it with a long encomium to a contemporary dramatist—the opera composer Richard Wagner. Nietzsche here claimed that Wagner's opera represented the rebirth of ancient Greek tragedy and would, if only given the chance, play the same healthful role in contemporary German culture that tragedy had played in ancient Greek culture.

The antagonistic reception this book received—which seems in retrospect entirely predictable, yet still hurt Nietzsche—drove down the number of students attending his lectures. When Nietzsche's health declined, the university was not at all averse to allowing him a permanent medical leave of absence and granting him a disability pension (small, but enough to live on). For most of the 1870's then, he was in and out of university life, eventually resigning for good in 1879.

Nietzsche had no fixed address for the remainder of his life. His illnesses—insomnia, indigestion, migraine headaches—made him hypersensitive to changes in the weather so that he was always in search of the perfect climate. Aided by the infrastructure of *Belle Epoque* tourism, which still brings Germans south in search of clear air and sunny skies, Nietzsche spent about a dozen years wandering among a variety of boarding houses, *pensiones* and furnished apartments. He became what the philosopher Gilles Deleuze calls a "philosophical nomad."[7] He would meet up with friends here and there and was an avid correspondent; but he lived very much alone for most of his later years, alone with his books and his thoughts, alone with his pills and his illnesses.

In winter, Nietzsche sought warmth. This led him to the Riviera, both the Italian and the French sections—hence Nice. In summer, Nietzsche sought cool air and low humidity. This led him to Switzerland—hence Sils-Maria. In between, he sought an elusive balance of temperature, humidity, barometric pressure, etc., which allowed him some sleep and relief from his migraines. Thus, he spent the springs and autumns of the 1870's and 1880's wandering across Switzerland and northern

7   See "Nomad Thought," in Allison 149

Italy, as far south as Sorrento and as far east as Venice, looking for the right combination of climatic conditions to suit his fragile health. He stayed here and there for varying lengths of time. He would often pull up stakes very suddenly when the weather or his mood changed. It was said he knew the Italian train system timetables by heart. Finally, he found what he considered the ideal conditions for the shoulder seasons in Turin, leading him to write the letter quoted above. But he was only able to enjoy this find for one spring and one fall.

He would sometimes venture as far north as parts of Germany, but rarely. And here comes the other half of the explanation of why this German philosopher worked almost exclusively as an expatriate. As a university student in the 1860's, he participated in that decade's upswing in German nationalism by joining a patriotic fraternity; he also enlisted in the military in 1867 (he was discharged in 1868 after sustaining an injury during a training exercise by being pitched forward onto the pommel of a horse). He served as a medical orderly in the Franco-Prussian War of 1870-71. But his reaction to the triumph of German unification at the end of that war was to rebel against it. His writings after 1876 are peppered with dismissive insults of Germany, German culture, the Kaiser, *Reichschancellor* Bismarck and so on. Here's an example from late 1888, written in Turin about ten days before his breakdown:

> And perhaps I could whisper something
> to my good Italians whom I *love* as much as
> I –. *Quosque tandem,* Crispi? Triple alliance:
> with the *Reich* an intelligent people can
> enter only a *mésalliance.*[8]

---

8   NCW Preface. This whole passage is a great example of how condensed, allusive and downright fun Nietzsche's writing is: A dash to create a deliberate

All this goes to explain why this German philosopher left Germany and spent the rest of his life wandering around southeastern France, northern Italy and the Swiss Engadine. But if Nietzsche wandered at least in part to flee German nationalism, one may ask how it is that he bears the reputation (still strong in some parts) of being a proto-Nazi.

Half of the answer is Nietzsche's erstwhile friendship with Richard Wagner. The opera composer Wagner, as is well-known, was a true proto-Nazi, someone who explicitly linked German nationalism with anti-Semitism, most notoriously in his opera *Die Meistersinger von Nürnberg*, an expressly patriotic work decrying foreign influence in German culture. The villain of *Die Meistersinger*, an officious busybody who insists singing be done in accordance with all the rules of musical composition which Wagner himself was busy breaking, is saddled by Wagner with Jewish stereotypes; for example, his final aria is a parody of the traditional Jewish liturgical melody, *Kal Nidrei*. This opera of infamy was Hitler's favorite for obvious reasons, although the unusually non-Wagnerian accessibility of the music may also have been part of its appeal.

At any rate, Nietzsche met Wagner in 1868, shortly before moving to Basel. Basel, as it happens, is not far from Lucerne, site of Tribschen, Wagner's residence at the time. Nietzsche visited so frequently that one of the guest rooms became known to the household as "the Professor's room." As already mentioned, Nietzsche's first book argued for Wagner's opera to be taken as the rebirth of ancient Greek tragedy in German form, but the influence between the two men went the other

gap to get the reader to fill in the rest of Nietzsche's thought out of the reader's own head (as much as he hates the Germans, right?), a bit of Latin to create some instant, ironic, mocking *gravitas* (to what end, Italian Prime Minister Crispi?), and finally a French term for a bad marriage that not only echoes the official name of the German-Austrian-Italian alliance but gives a quasi-comic tone, kind of like a Molière farce, to the supposedly serious business of international treaties.

way as well. Wagner had begun the famous *Ring* tetralogy back in the 1850's but had set it aside while working on other things. And though Wagner had long thought of his own work as a revival of ancient Greek tragedy, it was only after meeting Nietzsche that he returned to the project, finally completing it in 1874. They worked in concert for several years, defending each other in print. Nietzsche even wrote a pamphlet seeking to raise funds for Wagner's pet project— the establishment of a theater dedicated to his own works in Bayreuth.

However, the friendship *cum* partnership disintegrated between 1874 and 1877, and it had partly to do with anti-Semitism. Nietzsche became friendly with a man named Paul Rée, to whom Cosima Wagner (Richard's wife) refers in her account of the breakup: "Finally Israel intervened, in the form of a Dr. Rée, very sleek, very cool, at the same time as being wrapped up in Nietzsche and dominated by him, though actually outwitting him—the relationship between Judaea and Germany in miniature."[9] The fact that Rée's parents had long before his birth converted to Christianity to further their careers (this was necessary for advancement in many professions in Germany and Austria in the 19th and early 20th centuries), so that Rée himself was at most ethnically Jewish, proves that the Wagners' anti-Semitism was racial, not cultural or religious. It is not likely that Nietzsche originally befriended Rée precisely because of his Jewishness, but it is clear that he reveled in flaunting it in the Wagners' faces.

But why would he do that to his supposed friends? The answer may be that Nietzsche and Wagner were falling out already. In part, it may have been because Nietzsche had a crush on Cosima (this emerged in some letters written after

---

9   Hayman 204

the onset of his madness—"Ariadne," he called her).[10] But more likely it happened simply because these were two brilliant and ambitious men who had big plans not only for themselves but also for each other: Wagner saw Nietzsche as his ideological attack dog, while Nietzsche saw Wagner as an exemplar of the musical rebirth of German culture for which he advocated. Neither, of course, could long stand being a foot soldier in somebody else's culture war.

And so, in the same way that Nietzsche got off the German nationalist train just as it was reaching full speed, so too he left Wagner just as Wagner's project was succeeding. In *Ecce Homo* Nietzsche identifies the opening of the Bayreuth festival in 1876 as the tipping point.[11] There Nietzsche saw just what the supposed German cultural revival came to—a lot of jingoistic know–nothings loudly professing a love for German opera and German music, but really just seeking opportunities to feel good about themselves while eating lots of German *bratwurst* and drinking lots of German beer. There was plenty of fawning adulation of Wagner in Bayreuth as well, and it became clear to Nietzsche that what Wagner really wanted was the adulation, with the German cultural revival a distant second. Nietzsche left Bayreuth in disgust, claiming physical distress from the intellectual repulsion of what he had seen.[12]

To some extent this story is revisionist history, since there were lots of things going on in Nietzsche's philosophical development that pulled him away from Wagnerianism.[13] But

10 Hayman 335; see also letter to Burckhardt January 6, 1889, in *Portable Nietzsche* 687

11 EH books.HAH.2

12 Letter to Elisabeth, August 1, 1876 = Middleton #68.

13 For example, Nietzsche was coming to see science—which was anathema to Wagner—as necessary for culture to thrive, and thus came to think of culture as more cosmopolitan and less nationalistic than he had earlier. Interested readers may learn more about this from my first book, *Science, Culture, and Free Spirits,* (Prometheus, 2010).

whatever its cause, the fact that Nietzsche broke so decisively from Wagner before writing most of his philosophical works, in most of which there are aggressive, scathing criticisms of Wagner[14], along with frequent praise of Jews, Judaism, the Old Testament, etc.[15], raises the question why anyone could ever have thought he was a proto-Nazi also.

Enter Elisabeth Nietzsche. Younger by two years, always enamored of her brilliant older brother, Elisabeth loved that Nietzsche was friendly with the famous composer. She never understood why the relationship broke off. He brushed off her attempts to bring them back together, to return him to Bayreuth— "I belong to a different world," he wrote to her.[16] But she never let the matter alone. Not only did Wagner's celebrity status appeal to her, she genuinely partook of the ideology too. Nietzsche wasn't the Nazi in the family—Elisabeth was.

Elisabeth had married Bernhard Förster who, like his wife, believed Germany was too far gone with foreign—that is, Jewish—influence to be saved, and so it was necessary to renew the Aryan race somewhere uncontaminated. He chose Paraguay, and so he and Elisabeth moved there in 1886 with a bunch of fellow Aryans to found a colony called "Nueva Germania." Elisabeth unsuccessfully solicited money from Friedrich for it[17] (which in itself was odd since he had hardly any money of his own). Despite her efforts, the colony failed after Forster's suicide in 1889—though there are still a few German-speaking, German-named people living in that area, and a few of them even continue to maintain beliefs in Aryan superiority. [18]

---

14   See especially CW and NCW. The latter is composed of passages from other works, to which Nietzsche affixed a Preface declaring, "[W]e are antipodes."

15   HAH 475, GM III.22, etc.

16   Letter of February 3, 1882 = Middleton #93

17   Hayman, 303; for more on N's opposition to Förster, see letter to Elisabeth of May 20, 1884 = Middleton #134 & Kaufmann, 42-45

18   *New York Times* May 7, 2013

Elisabeth returned to Germany in December of 1890 and found her brother, who had lost his mind two years earlier, in the care of their mother, along with all of his notebooks. Nietzsche had given express instructions to his landlady to burn his notebooks should he die. But he hadn't died, he merely had a catastrophic mental breakdown, so the notebooks were returned to the family. On her return, Elisabeth was so determined to gain the rights to Nietzsche's literary estate she sued her own mother. She then published parts of her brother's notebooks, thus committing three crimes against him:

First, it was wrong to publish them at all, when he had insisted that they be burned. Elisabeth, left penniless after her husband's suicide (she and her mother were supported at this point only by Friedrich's pension from Basel), seems to have wanted to cash in on Nietzsche's rising fame.

Second, it was wrong to publish them under a title and according to an outline she found in one of the notebooks without knowing if this was Nietzsche's intention or just a passing thought. The result was the infamous book, *The Will to Power*. It's not at all clear Nietzsche would have gone through with either the title or the outline had he remained conscious—his notebooks are full of false starts and unfulfilled plans—and it's fairly certain that the notebook passages she put under this outline would have been rewritten and reshaped by Nietzsche had they been intended for publication. Most important, it is likely that he would have reorganized the passages in such a way that their placement in the whole would have been part of their message. The fact that the passages in *The Will to Power* are arranged mostly randomly has given later readers the impression that it's alright to read passages from *all* of Nietzsche's works, even the ones he published himself, in any order, out of context, without loss of content. Scholars of

Nietzsche still have to battle against this randomly selective way of reading his works.

And third, it was wrong to publish the notebooks after actually altering some of them, removing criticisms of his family and of the proto-Nazi movement. As Krell puts it, Elisabeth's editing "was carried out as much with scissors and a box of matches as with a pencil."[19] (This bowdlerizing has since been undone, and recent editions of Nietzsche's works contain the missing passages.)

But Elisabeth went further in promoting her brother's legacy. After hyphenating her family name onto her married name, Elisabeth Förster-Nietzsche set up the *Nietzsche Archiv* in Weimar, Germany, in 1896, and after the death of her mother in 1897 installed the broken shell of what had once been Nietzsche in it. She then set about riding the wave of Nietzsche's suddenly growing reputation. Part of the reason for his previous obscurity had been the radical novelty of his ideas and writing style. Another part of the problem had been an incompetent first publisher who failed to distribute Nietzsche's books properly and then went bankrupt. His readership during his conscious life was extremely small. His first big break came in the form of lectures about him at the University of Copenhagen in the Spring of 1888 by a Danish philosophy professor named Georg Brandes—a Jew, it should be pointed out, which should have raised a red flag for the proto-Nazi use of Nietzsche—and by the 1890's, Nietzsche was becoming well-known. So Elisabeth got all of his works re-issued and properly distributed, and the pathos of his dramatic breakdown helped to increase their sales.

The whole story is already sad and distasteful, but it actually gets worse: Nietzsche himself died in 1900 (that is, his body caught up with his long-dead mind), but his

---

19   Krell & Bates 53 fn.8

reputation as part of the German nationalist story grew to the point that German soldiers in World War I carried with them into battle not only the Bible but copies of *Thus Spoke Zarathustra*. (I don't know if any soldiers ever told stories about *Zarathustra* having stopped bullets and thus saving their lives.) Elisabeth herself, meanwhile, lived until 1935, long enough to invite the new *Reichschancellor* to tea, and the picture of Elisabeth welcoming Hitler at the door of the *Nietzsche Archiv* became famous. To further cement the connection between Nietzsche and Nazism, the Nazis installed in the chair of philosophy at the University of Berlin a man named Alfred Bäumler[20], who stood up to give his first lecture on Nietzsche and said that Nietzsche's true thoughts were not contained in his writings. He said this because, even with Elisabeth's aggressive editing, Nietzsche's writings in no way support fascism or anti-Semitism. But with a principle of interpretation so powerful—after all, you couldn't contradict what Bäumler said about Nietzsche because any appeal to Nietzsche's writings had already been ruled out—it was easy to show that Nietzsche was a true Nazi and that his greatness gave philosophical respectability to Nazism. This idea was then broadcast via Axis Sally to all the English and American soldiers fighting in World War II, so that by the end of the war the connection between Nietzsche and Nazism was so solid no one in the English-speaking world would touch Nietzsche.

It took Walter Kaufmann, one of Nietzsche's great rehabilitators, to unravel Elisabeth's machinations. Kaufmann, a German Jew who fled to America in 1938, was distressed to find Nietzsche in such disrepute. Kaufmann's book, published in 1950, thoroughly debunked the Nietzsche-Nazi connection and made a case for Nietzsche being worth

---

20 Kaufmann 40

the time of Anglophone readers. Kaufmann would go on to publish modern translations of most of Nietzsche's major works over the next twenty-five years, restoring the passages Elisabeth had cut. Then, in 1965, Arthur Danto published *Nietzsche as Philosopher*, making the case for Nietzsche's importance in philosophy (even today, some libraries shelve Nietzsche under German literature rather than philosophy), and in England at about the same time Reginald Hollingdale also published a book about Nietzsche, as well as several more translations. Gradually word got out.[21]

"Only the day after tomorrow belongs to me," wrote Nietzsche, regretting his small readership and anticipating the later impact of his ideas. "Some are born posthumously."[22] He was closer to the truth than he could have known.

---

21   My graduate advisor was Alexander Nehamas, who was a student of Kaufmann's at Princeton; the ripple effect of Kaufmann's work continues.
22   A Preface

On Our Way

AT WHAT POINT does a journey begin? From the moment you think of it? When you step out of the house? Or is it the moment roughly thirty years earlier when one of your professors is approved for leave, so that he is unavailable to advise your senior thesis on Martin Buber and as a result you write your thesis instead on Friedrich Nietzsche?

A case could be made for any of these (and many more). Nietzsche writes, in a passage about the eternal recurrence which we'll discuss at length later, "All things are so knotted together"[23] that any event inevitably has many causes and ramifications, and it is hard to pull these apart and locate a clear beginning.

For this trip, though, I choose to begin our journey with Julius Harvey.

Julius Harvey is the man who checks us through as we enter security. He is a big, jovial man, warm with his greetings to both us and the kids. He takes a look at our passports and has a bit of banter for each of us—about our pictures, our names, some kind of pleasantry.

This is the same Julius Harvey who checked us through Logan security four years earlier, in 2004, when we were on our way to London. Although it might come as a surprise that I can remember the name of a specific individual on the Logan Airport security staff four years after interacting with him for a mere minute or two, I remember him quite clearly because back then Julius Harvey made a point of telling our son Eli that he has a great middle name—Eli's middle name is Julius—and then pointing to his own name tag by way of explanation.

All this raises a thought about Nietzsche as traveler: In all his nomadic comings and goings, he must have run into the same railway officials, the same coach drivers, the same rail station eatery personnel over and over. Did he recognize them the way I recognized Julius Harvey? Did they recognize him, this nearly-blind eccentric with the outrageous mustache? All those anonymous encounters—did they become less anonymous for him, traversing the same territory back and forth, over and over, for a dozen years? Did he appreciate such people and such contacts or merely tolerate them? How would he have handled security check at Logan International would—he have responded to Julius Harvey's pleasantries?

"I love man," says Zarathustra[24], but as *Zarathustra* continues he quickly gets on the wrong side of a mindless crowd and soon declares, "To the hermits I shall sing my song, to the lonesome and the twosome."[25] And the ones and twos whom Nietzsche discusses in his writing are inevitably from elites of one kind or another:

> The time will come when ... one will regard not the masses but individuals, who form a kind of bridge across the turbulent stream of becoming ... as that republic of genius of which Schopenhauer once spoke; one giant calls to another across the desert intervals of time and, undisturbed by the excited chattering dwarfs who creep about

24   Z Prologue 2
25   Z Prologue 9

> beneath them, the exalted spirit-dialogue
> goes on.... [T]he goal of humanity cannot lie
> in its end but only in its highest exemplars.[26]

In terms of thinking about the history of philosophy, I'm fine with this. Like many in my profession, I want my students to recognize a "Great Conversation" of thinkers who speak from the context of their own historical situations but also speak across the centuries to each other—Descartes replying to Sextus Empiricus, Rawls thinking of Kant, and so on. Nietzsche makes, I think, a good case for how humanity's highest exemplars serve a crucial cultural purpose by inspiring us to be our best selves.[27] Outside of these exemplars, however (which include not only philosophers, but writers, artists, musicians, royalty, political leaders, military commanders and so on), there are in Nietzsche's world-view only herd-animals[28], conformists, "faded copies of great men produced on poor paper with worn-out plates"[29], "people of small minds"[30] who dare little and accomplish less.

Here I must disagree with Nietzsche. I have often been moved by people I've met who have nothing elite to point to in their resumés, yet who do their jobs with such effectiveness, and deal with their fellow humans with such warmth and genuineness, that they *do* make me feel glad to be human, at least as glad as the great ones I've met if not more, and who inspire me to be the best I can be. Like my car mechanic back in Farmington, for example—a genius at what he does, no exaggeration, and a *mensch* to boot. Sure, Julius Erving is an inspiration, likewise Julius Caesar and Julius "Groucho" Marx; but Julius Harvey is too. You walk away from an

26   UM II.9
27   UM III.1, see also BGE 257
28   BGE 199, 201, 202, et al
29   UM II.9
30   Z Prologue 5

encounter with him glad about life, glad to be a human being, glad even to be *this* human being, yourself.

Did Nietzsche never feel inspired by the humanity of the "ordinary" people around him? Perhaps, because of his nearsightedness, he never really saw them. At any rate, they don't enter into his writing, and while all his talk about Socrates and Frederick the Great and Goethe is heady and inspiring, I miss mention of the "ordinaries," since they're inspiring too.[31]

And at this point, putting my shoes back on after the security inspection, matching up again the rollaboards with the children doing the rolling, reassembling the lineup of the Professional Travelers and moving deeper into the concourse, I feel quite distant from Nietzsche, socially maladjusted elitist that he was. Why bother with those particular footsteps?

WE WANDER the long, wide concourses of Logan airport, crossing industrial carpeting under artificial light, distracted by flashy billboards with high-tech scrolling LED screens—a very different environment from the smoky train stations where Nietzsche would have been killing time, larger, cleaner, quieter, yet somehow more impersonal as well. We've got plenty of time (in part because of the welcome efficiency of people like Julius Harvey), so I exchange some dollars to euros to be able to hit the ground running in Europe.

Finding supper at the airport food court is somewhat more complicated than one might think. For one thing, we keep kosher, which means not only that we avoid pork and shellfish

---

31   A possible exception is Nietzsche's love for Bizet's great opera *Carmen*, the lead roles for which are a gypsy, a soldier, and a bullfighter, all of whom, despite their humble stations, evince nobility of character. But this, of course, is a work of art, not a live person.

but also any other form of meat when we eat out, since we can't know it was prepared in accordance with the regulations for *kashrut*. In addition, many seemingly non-meat foods include some form of meat ingredient. For example, most restaurant soups are made from chicken or beef stock, baked beans usually have lard, etc. So we read menus carefully and ask questions. The result is a certain hesitancy before eating.

We're far from the only people to eat this way, of course: all vegetarians and vegans, as well as anyone on a restricted diet of any kind, develop the same habitual suspicion. Indeed, we're relatively liberal among those who keep *kosher*. Many would not eat any hot food at a restaurant at all, since the expansion induced by the heating process presumably allows non-kosher food particles left on cooking utensils and dishes to be absorbed by the vegetarian food being prepared. Many observant Jews would not eat restaurant food at all unless the restaurant was under rabbinical supervision. Our feeling is that compromises must be made to be engaged with the world, and we're willing to take what we feel are minor risks with our *kashrut* observance to do so.

Nietzsche, the philosophical nomad, had no choice about eating other people's cooking, and he developed a strong sense of suspicion all his own. Living at a time when vegetarianism was growing in German-speaking areas, he was a vegetarian himself for a brief period in his twenties, apparently for moral reasons. But he soon gave it up, either on the recommendation of a doctor or at Wagner's urging; it's not clear. Years later, he went to the other extreme, expressing suspicion of vegetarianism:

> A diet that consists predominantly of
> rice leads to the use of opium and narcotics,
> just as a diet that consists predominantly

> of potatoes leads to the use of liquor. But it also has ... narcotic effects.... [T]hose who promote narcotic ways of thinking and feelings, like some Indian gurus, praise a diet that is entirely vegetarian and would like to impose that as a law upon the masses. In this way they want to create and increase the need that they are in a position to satisfy.[32]

The stereotypes about East Asians and East Europeans are embarrassing, but the idea that religious leaders promote the condition which they themselves then claim to relieve anticipates one of Nietzsche's many provocative criticisms of Christianity, namely that what priests do is blame the sufferers for their suffering—i.e. get them to interpret their suffering as resulting from their "guilt"—so that they, the priests, make themselves indispensable for their flocks' absolution. [33] It's interesting too that Nietzsche might have unwittingly stumbled onto what modern nutrition recommends concerning the importance of not neglecting dietary protein. I suspect, though, that what was uppermost in his mind as he wrote this passage was his own condition when he first fell under Wagner's spell.

At any rate, much more important to his dietary regimen was his health. He was prone to digestive problems, and these could concatenate into migraines and/or insomnia. He became extremely careful about what he ate as time went on. The German writer Stefan Zweig, in his biography of Nietzsche, paints the following picture:

> Carefully the myopic man sits down to a table; carefully, the man with the sensitive

---

32   GS 145
33   See GM III.

> stomach considers every item on the menu:
> whether the tea is not too strong, the food
> not spiced too much, for every mistake in his
> diet upsets his sensitive digestion, and every
> transgression in his nourishment wreaks
> havoc with his quivering nerves for days. No
> glass of wine, no glass of beer, no alcohol, no
> coffee at his place, no cigar and no cigarette
> after his meal, nothing that stimulates,
> refreshes, or rests him .... [34]

Nietzsche surely felt the same suspicion of food and had the same sense of separation from the world which I associate with *kashrut*. The distinction between what's outside one's body and what one will allow to enter becomes terribly important. One holds the world at arm's length, inspecting it. We see Nietzsche doing it throughout his life, and maybe I do it a little bit too. If anything, he was even more careful than I am, since a mistake in his diet led to consequences much more severe than a few minutes' penance on Yom Kippur.

In a way, Nietzsche's situation is not that unusual—many people have dietary restrictions based on health. I have some of my own: I need to watch my cholesterol, and I'm somewhat sensitive to lactose. So I should be patronizing the Wok and Roll stand that offers tofu. But my family is excited about Sbarro, so I wind up with stromboli instead. As we unwrap our food, steaming warm, I'm feeling remorse. Having had quiche yesterday, and leftover quiche for lunch today, I've actually had a lot of cheese in the last few meals and thus greatly violated my personal regimen. Digestive trouble on the plane will be unpleasant and while the consequences (if any) of too much cholesterol are years away rather than immediate migraines, still, I didn't need to be so careless.

34   Quoted in the *Portable Nietzsche* 104

I've compromised my own regimen in order to go with the crowd—the most basic sin there is in Nietzsche's view. The mustachioed Jiminy Cricket on my shoulder pipes up:

> In his heart every man knows quite well that, being unique, he will be in the world only once and that no imaginable chance will for a second time gather together into a unity so strangely variegated an assortment as he is: he knows it but he hides it like a bad conscience.... [W]hat is it that constrains the individual...to think and act like a member of the herd...? With the great majority it is indolence, inertia, in short... laziness.[35]

Well, that names my tune—it was easier to buy from one place instead of two, that's all. It's a small thing, sure, but I did go with the crowd, in the sense that I let other people's preferences be my guide instead of sticking with my own inner compass.

And maybe in my life I've gone with the crowd in other, much bigger ways: staying Jewish, marrying, having a family, things that lots of people do. This is one of the chief respects in which I worry about being unfaithful to his footsteps: Have I neglected Nietzsche's call to be an individual, which I've always found so inspiring?

> No one can construct for you the bridge upon which precisely you must cross the stream of life, no one but you yourself alone. There are, to be sure, countless paths and bridges and demi-gods which would bear

---

> you through this stream, but only at the cost
> of yourself: you would put yourself in pawn
> and lose yourself. There exists in the world
> a single path along which no one can go
> except you: whither does it lead? [36]

Nietzsche's philosophy of individualism developed originally in the context of his project of German cultural revival. While most Germans took the unification of the 1870's in the direction of political nationhood, Nietzsche focused on the needs of culture. Culture is important, he argued, because of its benefits for the development and education of creative individuals. And creative individuals are important because they produce new culture. The relationship is manifestly circular and recognizes the interdependence of individuals and their culture.

As Nietzsche's career progressed, he began focusing less on general culture and more on what it takes to educate and inspire culturally creative individuals. He attempted to do a lot of that educating and inspiring himself in his writing. Free spirits, strong individuals, higher men—whatever he calls them, the idea is always to get them—us—to construct our own "culture of one" (as I like to call it). Just as in his early writings he describes ideal national culture as "unity of style,"[37] in his later writings he urges individuals to "give style to your character."[38] The credo he professes is, "My judgment is my judgment—no one else is easily entitled to it,"[39] and he couples this attitude with a challenge to the reader: "This is my way…where is yours?"[40]

---

36   UM III.1
37   UM I.1
38   GS 290
39   BGE 43
40   Z III.11

[F]orward on the path of wisdom with a bold step and full of confidence! However you may be, serve yourself as your own source of experience! Throw off discontent with your nature, forgive yourself your own ego, for in any event you possess in yourself a ladder with a hundred rungs upon which you can climb to knowledge.[41]

It is difficult under any circumstances to undo the layers of socialization and find the "real" individual underneath. But for those of us who, unlike Nietzsche, are socially well-adjusted, it's especially difficult. Although we pity his lonely, sickly life, he lived in his own, self-created world, relatively undisturbed by outside claims on his time or his consciousness.

Such as, for example, my family noticing that several foreign cities and their mileage from Boston are posted on the wall of the food court.

"Which is farther from Boston, London or Paris?" asks Vicky. "And no fair looking."

Rosie starts, "I'll go with Paris."

"Yep, it's Paris, 3449 miles to 3284. OK, how about Paris versus Amsterdam?"

"Oh, tough one. Sam?"

"Um, nope—too close to call."

"Amsterdam, just barely, 3461 to 3449."

"Well, but what if you take a shortcut?" Eli, of course.

Nietzsche was a decent geographer too, nomad that he was. In the same letter I quoted earlier, in which he identifies Nice, Turin and Sils as the three perfect places for him to spend his year, he explains why that is:

---

41   UM III.1

> What convinces me is the air, the dry air, which is the same in all three places, and for the same meteorological reasons: snow-capped mountains to the north and west. That is the calculation that has brought me here [i.e. to Turin], and I am enchanted! Even on the very warm days—and we have had such already—that famous Zephyr blows, of which I had heard only the poets speak (without believing them: pack of liars!). The nights are cool. From the middle of the city you can see the snow.[42]

Nietzsche's joy in this realization is like ours playing the distance game—delight in geography is a delight in the earth itself. "Remain faithful to the earth, my brothers,"[43] says Zarathustra. Some scholars take this line to show Nietzsche anticipating deep ecology, but I think that's just anachronistic. All he means is to care about "this" world rather than devalue it in favor of a "next" world, or to care about the material world of our senses rather than an immaterial world of pure ideas. It's about affirmation of the here and now, life as actually lived, the corporeal, the earthly.

Odd place to think of loving the earth—in the middle of a fast food court, in the middle of a vast complex of steel and concrete, in the middle of seventeen thousand acres of paved runways and hangars, about to board a giant hunk of metal which is burning fossil fuel and spewing fumes. Would Nietzsche be appalled? Possibly. But at the same time, it's this whole artificial, inorganic construction which allows us to step off the earth in North America and step onto it again

---

42 Letter to Reinhart von Seydlitz, May 13, 1888, Krell & Bates 224
43 Z I.22.2

in Europe just a few hours later.

Eventually we throw out our supper remains and roll down the concourse to the departure gates. Amid the rolling wheels I hear his voice on my shoulder again:

> Alas, where shall I climb now with my longing? From all mountains I look out for fatherlands and motherlands. But home I found nowhere; a fugitive am I in all cities and a departure at all gates. [44]

"A departure at all gates"—good motto for an airport, I'd say.

And so it happens that, as we walk down the ramp, step out of Logan Airport, and step into the sky, he is with me as he always is. The seven of us settle into the six seats reserved for us, and we're off.

---

44 Z II.14

Amor Fati and *Ressentiment* in Bavaria

DESPITE VICKY'S urging, the kids hardly sleep. The in-flight movies are too tempting for the boys, and the girls curl up with their books. There's a certain joy in setting up one's seat area and then living in one's little private space for a few hours. Maybe Nietzsche enjoyed this part of his many relocations, the joy of continually reconstructing his own little world in a new place.

I wake to the greenness of Bavaria in the summer. The new airport is well outside the city in the midst of beautiful farmland. Munich, it must be said, does not play much of a part in Nietzsche's story. He did see Wagner's *Tristan und Isolde* here in 1872, twice in three days. This may seem excessive; but considering he couldn't buy the CD or download it, paying admission a second time was the only way to hear it again. He did not return, however, until the autumn of 1885, when he visited a friend, Reinhard von Seydlitz, and flirted with his wife, Irene—"I almost talked to her in the second person singular,"[45] he confesses in a letter, thrilled and mortified by his forwardness. He stopped in again in the spring of 1886, on his way to visit his mother, to try to persuade a conductor to perform an opera by his friend Peter Gast (unsuccessfully). Otherwise, Munich was for Nietzsche just a place to change trains.

We, likewise, are just changing planes. With a five-hour and forty-minute layover, we had briefly entertained thoughts of going into Munich itself and getting a quick tour, but the distance from the city means we'd have spent most of our time in transit, so it wouldn't really be worth it. There's an amusement park nearby, but we decide there wouldn't be much point in that either. So instead we stay at the airport, just hanging out, as surely he did at train stations so often during his peregrinations. One thing we're sure of, in terms of adjusting to a new time zone, is that we need to get out into the natural light quickly to readjust our circadian clocks. So as soon as we land and use bathrooms, we begin our layover by walking outdoors, rollaboards in tow.

The highpoint of our light-absorbing walk is the Hotel Kempinsky just outside the terminal. Its atrium is entirely glass, allowing one to see that a series of columns hung with flower baskets, which begins outside the hotel, continues inside the atrium along exactly the same line. It's quite striking. Having walked in the heat for a while now, we are grateful for the comfortable seats and air conditioning. To complete our joy, the barman graciously agrees to fill up our water bottles from his tap.

I feel a little out of place, luxuriating in the lobby of a swanky hotel when we're trying to travel economically. The elegant surroundings feel suitable to the noble side of my nature, but to actually be able to afford such a place I'd have had to have made different choices long ago. And it's actually a respect in which to feel communion with Herr Doctor ex-Professor Nietzsche, who camped out in some of Europe's classiest tourist destinations during the *Belle Epoque* armed with only his limited disability pension from the university and occasional gifts from his mother, themselves derived from his father's meager death benefits. He was, as a friend of mine once put it, "independently poor"—he had enough money to live on, but only by being frugal, cautiously recording his expenses in his notebooks, and counting his change.

It's an aspect of Nietzsche's life that surfaces not in his published writings but in his letters, such as this one to his mother from Nice during his last stay there:

> My dear mother: The money you sent and your accompanying letter brought me great pleasure—almost as if you had made me a present. My finances were in rather a bad way; and perhaps I have already told you that my hotel fees have been increased this winter.[46]

He doesn't mean hotel room charges—his residence was always a boarding house, *pension*, or small apartment—but he did take one meal a day in a hotel pretty much everywhere he lived. I sometimes wonder how he felt as he looked around the dining room at people actually staying in the hotel, as opposed to returning to down-market lodgings the way he did. Did he ever feel any *ressentiment* towards them? *Ressentiment* is the word Nietzsche uses (in French) in *On the Genealogy of Morals* for the resentment felt by the weak (the "slaves") concerning the powerful (the "masters"), the feeling which he says gives rise to the standard morality of our day, the morality which praises humility and helpfulness while condemning swagger and egotism.

> While every noble morality develops from a triumphant affirmation of itself, slave morality from the outset says No to what

---

46   Letter of March 20, 1888; Middleton #166

is 'outside,' what is 'different,' what is 'not itself,' and *this* No is its creative deed. This inversion of the value-positing eye—this *need* to direct one's view outward instead of back to oneself—is of the essence of *ressentiment:* in order to exist, slave morality always first needs a hostile external world; it needs, physiologically speaking, external stimuli in order to act at all—its action is fundamentally reaction.[47]

Ressentiment implicitly contains the view of oneself as a loser and the world as a vale of tears, and thus leads one either to not care enough about it to live creatively or else to create in a bitter spirit that will drag others down too. Nietzsche locates the source of healthy creativity in what he calls *amor fati.* The phrase alludes to Spinoza's slogan, *amor dei,* and is clearly meant to replace it in the post-religious world Nietzsche anticipates: "My formula for greatness in a human being is *amor fati*: that one wants nothing to be different, not forward, not backward, not in all eternity. Not merely bear what is necessary, still less conceal it ... but *love* it."[48] It is only in loving your situation and believing in yourself, according to him, that you can create cultural tokens that perpetuate that feeling, and that's what your culture needs, not the spreading of your *ressentiment.*

Did Nietzsche never feel *ressentiment*? His published writings never betray that mood and in his letters he usually takes a brave pose, even with his mother. The remainder of the letter quoted above gives a wonderful sense of what daily life was like for him:

---

47   GM I.10
48   EH clever.10

Nevertheless, my circumstances here are significantly less costly than those of the average hotel guest; and, moreover, this winter I have what I did not have before – a room which I like, a high one, with excellent light for my eyes, freshly decorated, with a large, heavy table, chaise longue, bookcase, and dark reddish-brown wallpaper, which I chose myself. It still seems to me that I must hold on to Nice: the climate has a better influence on me than any other. Precisely here I can use my eyes twice as much as anywhere else. Under this sky my head has become more free, year by year; here the uncanny consequences of being ill for years on end, in the proximity and expectation of death, are more mild in their effects. I would also mention that my digestion is better here than elsewhere; but above all, my mind feels more alert here, and carries its burden more easily—I mean the burden of a fate to which a *philosopher* is inevitably condemned. I walk for an hour every morning, in the afternoon for an average of three hours, and at a rapid pace—the same walk day after day—it is beautiful enough for that. After supper, I sit until nine o'clock in the dining room, in company mainly with Englishmen and English ladies, with a lamp, which has a shade, at my table. I get up at six-thirty in the morning and make my own tea and also have a few biscuits. At twelve noon I have breakfast; at six, the main meal of the day. No wine, no beer, no spirits, no coffee—

the greatest regularity in my mode of living and in my diet. Since last summer I have accustomed myself to drinking water—a good sign, a step forward. It happens that I have just been ill for three days; today everything is all right again.[49]

Perhaps Nietzsche never succumbed totally to *ressentiment,* but my guess is that he did occasionally feel it, and my evidence is that his writings show he recognized the positive value in rooting it out of himself. Here is the first published mention of *amor fati,* in what Nietzsche calls his New Year's resolution for 1882:

I want to learn more and more to see as beautiful what is necessary in things; then I shall be one of those who make things beautiful. *Amor fati*: let that be my love henceforth! I do not want to wage war on what is ugly. I do not want to accuse; I do not even want to accuse those who accuse. *Looking away* shall be my only negation. And all in all and on the whole: someday I wish to be only a Yes-sayer.[50]

To make the world more beautiful it suffices to *perceive* the world as beautiful. That in itself is a beautiful thought, and Nietzsche's success in doing this in much of his writing is part of why I love him.[51]

---

49   Middleton #166
50   GS 276
51   It is also why I have stuck so closely, in writing this memoir, to our actual travels. Though it has often been tempting to rearrange or even make up episodes, I have been guided by the idea that This Is How It Happened, and as a lover of fate I have affirmed How It Happened and remained faithful to that.

Perspectivism in Nice

WE LAND in Nice and run out of the airport to catch a bus to the city and find it takes us only as far as the train station. We walk and roll from there to Avenue Jean Médecin (named after a long-time mayor of Nice). Reaching the avenue, we step into the future.

I could also have said that we step onto a tram, but that wouldn't describe the experience. The tram is part of the Ligne d'Azur, the public transportation network for the Cote d'Azur. And it is a marvel: brand-new in November 2007, it is only in its eighth month of operation when we board it. It is quiet, roomy, smooth-running and most of all, incredibly beautiful. The forward line of the front car (which is the same as the rearward line of the last car—there is no turning circle, so it just reverses direction at the end of the line) is a perfect hyperbola set off by the curve of the semicircle of glass which forms the first passenger window. With its gleaming silver and bronze exterior paneling and its smooth, almost silent running, the tram is a ghost from the future.

The stepping-into-the-future experience on the tram in Nice is striking, partly because of the aesthetics of the design, partly because the smoothness of the ride soothes the travelers' weary bones at the end of a long day, and partly because of the setting: From Avenue Jean Médecin the twenty-first century tram enters the eighteenth century Place Massena.

Place Massena (named after one of Napoleon's generals, born here in Nice in 1758) is not the geographic center of Nice, but it functions as Nice's center of gravity, standing between and thus connecting the old city and the new, the tourist hotels and the business district. Avenue Jean Médecin enters from the north, between Rue Gioffredo and Rue Massena. There is a fountain with a classical-style statue in the center and four horses around it at the southern end. To the east and the west of the fountain, the *place* opens onto parks lining Boulevard Jean Jaurès, Avenue Félix Faure, Avenue de Verdun and the Avenue des Phocéens, themselves dotted with even more fountains. Handsome three-and-four-story brick buildings with arcade-covered shops at ground level and topped with dormers form the *place*'s four sides. Before them stand light poles, as tall as the buildings, in the style of old gas lamps. Additional poles, also as tall as the buildings, hold incongruous, double-take-inducing, larger-than-life, all-white human figures in various positions of sitting, standing, kneeling and so on. The whole thing is paved so that pedestrians, unencumbered by paths, can stroll in any direction they please. Place Massena thus mixes paving with flowers, open space with shops, people with water, whimsical art with serious history.

The *place* itself is paved in a checkerboard pattern, but with alternating lines angled off-kilter and then reversing their angles every other panel. Looking out to the edges along the straight lines, the paving looks like a checkerboard. Looking down at the area at your feet, you see a jaunty crazy quilt. Then if you look out to the edges at a forty-five-degree angle, you get a bizarre visual illusion of diamonds that won't stand still. It's quite clever and endlessly fascinating.

The way the paving looks different depending on where

you're standing and which direction you're looking is a nice illustration of Nietzsche's way of thinking about truth and knowledge, which has come to be known as perspectivism. For many scholars this is his most important contribution to philosophy and an idea that I often find relevant in life.

The basic idea of perspectivism is that values and truths depend on the perspective of the person holding or believing them in very much the same way that physical things appear differently depending on one's visual vantage point. Any idea human beings have is necessarily shaped by their background, experiences, assumptions, cultural framework, etc.—their standpoint, we often say—as well as what their purposes are (often unconscious).

> Gradually it has become clear to me what every great philosophy so far has been: namely the personal confession of its author and a kind of involuntary and unconscious memoir; also that the moral (and immoral) intentions in every philosophy constituted the real germ of life from which the whole plant had grown.[52]

If this is true of philosophers who are supposed to be able to transcend such things and be impartially rational, it is surely true of everyone. Nietzsche here focuses on where people are coming from and where they're going (their experiences and their intentions). But notice that even when two people share a lot of background and/or purpose—stand in the same place, we might say—they might not see things the same way. This is most obvious with regard to color: Some people are color-blind and insist that to say the barn "is" red

---

52   BGE 6

or the grass "is" green is to make an unjustified claim about reality. Even people with supposedly full color vision disagree about colors. For years Vicky and I disagreed about whether the plaid of my fall coat was blue or green. And remember that kerfuffle on the Internet and in the media, which arose a couple years after we had returned and I was revising this manuscript, about a photo of a dress that clearly looked blue and black to some people and clearly looked white and gold to others. Even when two people do agree on what to call a color, they can never be sure they're experiencing it the same way. Perspective, says Nietzsche, is "the basic condition of life."[53]

When this idea is applied to truth, the sense of the word "perspective" is no longer strictly visual, but the phenomenon is the same – when you take a new conceptual vantage point (i.e. try a new idea), you look at (i.e. think about) things differently. And so what seems true to me, from my perspective, seems false to you, from yours, and so truth is relative to perspective.

Now some will argue that while people may disagree about *some* things, other things are simply facts. The paving on Place Massena, for example, complex and visual-illusion-inducing as it is, nevertheless does have a definite configuration. That is, the paving has definite structure and composition—straight lines here, angled lines there, white concrete here, black concrete there, etc. No amount of color-blindness or disagreement between people will change that. The white plastic people on top of the posts, too—there's no reason to doubt that they're there, or that one is kneeling, another sitting cross-legged and so on.

Nietzsche is actually happy to call such things facts. This is a bit surprising, since perspectivism implies that nothing is immutably true and thus there can be no facts in the traditional sense. However, there can still be facts in the sense of the best views available, views that are extremely well-attested, products of long, sober investigation using the best methods, frequently cross-checked by multiple people— things on which disagreement is hard to imagine. And this is the sense in which Nietzsche continues to use the term, for example when he praises the culture of Greco-Roman antiquity for having developed "the sense for facts, the last and most valuable of all the senses."[54]

Notice though, that even such extremely well-attested views are still human views, still utilizing the human perceptual apparatus and thus still perspectival. Even the most indisputable view is also constructed from a certain perspective. "We behold all things through the human head and cannot cut off this head, while the question nonetheless remains what of the world would still be there if one had cut it off."[55] For us humans, there is no such thing as truth that transcends human limitations.

> How far the perspective character
> of existence extends or indeed whether
> existence has any other character than this;
> whether existence without interpretation,
> without 'sense,' does not become 'nonsense;'
> whether, on the other hand, all existence
> is not essentially actively engaged in

54 A 59. Thus one of his most famous lines, "Facts are precisely what there are not, only interpretations," cannot be taken to be his considered view. It's important to recognize that this line comes from one of the notebooks that Elizabeth published after his breakdown (as aphorism 481 in *The Will to Power*), whereas Nietzsche uses the word "fact" often in his published writing. To privilege the notebook line over the published uses of the word "fact" is to do him a disservice, even if the unpublished line does, admittedly, help us understand what he's driving at—no facts in the traditional sense of something that's absolutely and unconditionally true, only perspectival interpretations.

55 HAH 9

interpretation—that cannot be decided even by the most industrious and most scrupulously conscientious analysis and self-examination of the intellect; for in the course of this analysis the human intellect cannot avoid seeing itself in its own perspectives and *only* in these. We cannot look around our own corner: it is a hopeless curiosity that wants to know what other kinds of intellects and perspectives there *might* be....[56]

No matter how hard you try, you'll still be a human being and so still be looking at things and thinking about things from a certain psychological/social/cultural vantage point and utilizing a certain physiologically and historically conditioned perceptual apparatus. Even if one works with other people as hard as one can and comes to an agreement, falsity always remains possible—even if seven billion people agree on the truth of a fact, it's always possible that it will have to be revised, as facts often are in the course of scientific advances. Thus "physics, too, is only an interpretation and exegesis of the world."[57] And thus there's no such thing as absolute truth, that is, something that's true regardless of perspective.

For anyone who has previously lived unreflectively assuming there is a single, unchanging truth about everything—a view Nietzsche himself held in his earliest works, but later calls "dogmatism"[58]—perspectivism is quite unsettling. In Nietzsche's day, with universalist Christianity, Victorian moralism and other absolutist views still ascendant in Europe, perspectivism came across as a wild, radical and dangerous view. An early reviewer of *Beyond Good and Evil*

---

56   GS 374
57   BGE 14
58   BGE Preface

said the book should be marked with black flags the way the dynamite being used to blast the Gotthard tunnel was.[59] Nietzsche loved that, as you can imagine, and proudly crowed in *Ecce Homo*, "I am no man, I am dynamite."[60] In our day though, the idea that we need to pay attention to people's psychological/sociological/cultural assumptions has become almost trite—to such an extent have we all followed in Nietzsche's footsteps, most of us unknowingly. Nowadays we *expect* news accounts to be slanted, and we expect people's views of reality to conflict, since most of us don't think there can be such a thing as impartiality.

So perspectivism in our day actually cuts in the other direction from what it did when Nietzsche was alive. And that's because Nietzsche is *not* giving up on truth entirely (that is, he is not, in philosophical terms, a relativist). He doesn't say there's no such thing as truth; he says truth depends on perspective. So what one can do in cases of disagreement is either try to find some third perspective which decides between the two, or get one of the two people to adopt the other's perspective and see that it is better than the perspective s/he started with. So, for example, if one wanted to recreate the paving in Place Massena for one's little town (take note, Farmington Board of Selectmen), and one disagrees with the person hired to pour the concrete about how it's laid out, one can visit the site and observe it closely to see the proper angles, etc., and discuss it until agreement is reached. In this case, we would say that the two people having a disagreement came to share a perspective. Or it might be that to settle their dispute they have to move to a third perspective, that is, take a view different from where both of them began, but a place from which they can now come to an agreement.

59   J.V. Widmann, review of BGE, quoted by Nietzsche in a letter to Malwida von Meysenbug, September 24, 1886 = Middleton #145
60   EH destiny.1

Notice that whatever one does to establish facts limits one's perspective. Leaning down and touching the pavement with one's finger might help one understand how the concrete was poured, but it won't allow one to see the checkerboard pattern—for that one has to stand up and look away rather than down. And looking along the lines to see the checkerboard pattern doesn't allow one to see the shimmering diamonds that appear at a forty-five-degree angle. So which of these is the "right" way to look at the paving—down, straight, at an angle? Even if one goes up in a helicopter and takes a photo from above, or uses satellite view to get the whole *place* in one view (a secular version of what philosophers call a "God's-eye view"), one hasn't actually gotten *all* of it, because one hasn't gotten the view from person-height at which the visual illusions operate. No one of these views is the single right one. Nor can one say that all of them together constitute the truth of the object because, on the one hand, more can always be generated, and on the other hand, one can't actually hold all the views simultaneously—you can't look at the pavement from up close and from helicopter height at the same time. Think of cubist painters, such as Picasso, trying to cram all the possible perspectives of something into a single painting. The more views one has of something, the better one's understanding of it will be, certainly. But "better" is different from "best"—whatever the situation, there's no one perspective that's privileged, no "right" one that will work in every single case. Sometimes one must get closer to something to get a better view of it, while at other times one has to move farther away. For some purposes one will want to think of things physically, scientifically, materially; and at others it will be more accurate to think of them spiritually, poetically, conceptually. For any given purpose, there are better and worse places from which to view something. Just as we need to know where people are coming from in order to understand their perspective, we have to know where they are going as well. Once we do that, though, we can both come to an agreement.

Thus, despite his reputation as a relativist, Nietzsche is still fighting for truth. And although in his own day he was seen as undermining the authoritative truths that many Europeans still believed in, in our day a large part of what's valuable about perspectivism (in *my* view) is that it actually sticks up for and provides a way to understand the idea that one *can* adjudicate disputes, *can* discuss values, *can* strive to find a better, third view. Rather than just throw up our hands and say, "Oh, everyone's got their own opinion," we can recognize that some opinions are better than others. Rather than say that every aspect of the news media is slanted, we can recognize that some reporters are trying to get the story right rather than using it to further their own agenda, and that someone who is at least *trying* to get the story right will probably offer us a better perspective than someone who is deliberately trying to spin us.

Of course, even a view that has been arrived at by someone attempting to be impartial is still just a perspective and as such is still subject to being confronted by yet another perspective that casts it into doubt. Thus, perspectivism conveys a view of truth which sees the quest for truth as never-ending. Above I quoted part of a passage entitled *"Our new infinite"*; it continues as follows:

> I should think that today we are at least far from the ridiculous immodesty that would be involved in decreeing from our corner that perspectives are permitted only from this corner. Rather has the

> world become 'infinite' for us all over again,
> inasmuch as we cannot reject the possibility
> that *it may include infinite interpretations.*[61]

There can never be a final, ultimate, perfect perspective that answers all questions, satisfies all possible needs, purposes and values and provides unchanging truth. There's no vantage point that can satisfy all perspectives and so we must keep looking, keep comparing and keep discussing.

This is the most important point, the one that distinguishes perspectivism from both absolutism and relativism. If you're an absolutist there's no point in talking things over, because when one person has the truth, it's the *Truth* (that's the "ridiculous immodesty" of the above passage). But the same is true for relativism—if one opinion is as good as any other, why bother trying to convince anyone of anything, and why bother listening to anyone else? Nietzsche doesn't talk about this side of things because in his day, he saw the crucial battle to be the one against absolutism. In our day, it could be argued, the battle against relativism is equally pressing. Either way, for perspectivism further discussion is always potentially valuable, because there could always be some new perspective one hasn't considered, or some new way to look at things, or some new way to compare two different opinions. Perspectivism is thus a perpetual invitation to discussion.[62]

And what of Nietzsche's view itself? Absolutists are often

---

61   GS 374

62   In the years following our trip, there's been a lot of frustration in the US about how partisan differences in Washington have become more and more intractable. One could blame Nietzsche for fomenting the view that people's views are determined by their backgrounds, and thus there's a Democratic view of reality, and a Republican view of reality, and never the twain shall meet. But in fact perspectivism implies possible resolution of disputes, since we can always adopt new perspectives, either the one held by those disputing with us or "third" ones that both of us must move to in order to resolve our differences and come to see things the same way. What it takes is openness to listen to another's view, willingness to explain one's own, and readiness to move to a better one.

tempted to reply petulantly that, by Nietzsche's own lights, all this is just Nietzsche's interpretation, Nietzsche's perspective. But Nietzsche, as usual, is several steps ahead: "Supposing that this also is only interpretation—and you will be eager enough to make this objection?—well, so much the better."[63] Nietzsche's perspectivism is a perspective too, of course! What else could it be? So the view is consistent. And if you don't like Nietzsche's perspective—come up with a better one!

AT the southern end of Place Massena, the tram makes a ninety degree turn to the east and heads down Boulevard Jean Jaurès. We get off at the Gare Routière. We have a vague sense of where our apartment is and we start walking in what we believe to be the right direction, looking for street signs, but as we wander across the park between the two lanes of the *boulevard*, a woman we've never seen before blurts out "Are you Mrs. Cohen?" We're taken aback by her picking Vicky out and by her addressing us in English, but really, how many families of six would there be at that hour looking for street signs? Sure enough, it is our apartment manager Joy, an Englishwoman who lives in Nice and manages apartments for the many Englishmen and women who own second homes here.

The English were among the first tourists of the modern era to visit Nice. For one thing, the Industrial Revolution created a middle-class with the wealth and means to move about. For another, English seafaring history made them comfortable with the idea of getting on boats and going long distances. Empire helped too, bringing the sense that they owned the world and might as well go see it from time to

time. Where to go, exactly? Given the damp, gray—excuse
me, *grey*—climate in the British Isles, the English naturally
sought the Riviera. Combine these facts and it becomes clear
why Nice's coastal boulevard, lined with deluxe hotels, is
called the Promenade des Anglais. Nietzsche mentions it in
several letters; he liked to walk westward in the afternoon,
then return with the setting sun at his back lighting up the
hotels and the old city before him.[64]

Joy guides us to our temporary home. Rue de Gubernatis
is a narrow street and our building is fairly ordinary looking,
but when we reach our apartment it is light and airy and has
been well-renovated. It has all the "mod cons," as Joy puts
it—dishwasher and clothes washer and microwave and air
conditioning. The rear looks out on a garden courtyard; the
front on the shutters across the street.

A moment to describe the shutters of Nice, which in
retrospect, I think are the town's defining feature. Most
buildings have them, even the newer ones. The shutters are
tall and have thin wooden slats. They swing open sideways,
but also have a central section that can swing out like an
awning. It's a clever design, answering to the Riviera's two
contradictory needs: to shield from the sun and to let in the
breeze. Most of the shutters are in need of paint, but that only
adds to their charm. These shutters express Nice's age and
speak to an atmosphere of gentle neglect—a sense of living in
the past, of trying to maintain a connection to a certain time.

Once I have a base, I can relax and appreciate my
surroundings. Nietzsche was similar, I believe. Transitions
often made him ill, and thus his medical need to change
residences was bad for his health, paradoxically. But once
he had slept—and walked—in a new place, he recovered his
esprit. Of course, that was only until the season changed and

---

64   See Krell & Bates 189.

he had to find a new place, less hot, less humid, less whatever. Still, I can understand how he could successfully live as a nomad—a temporary home is a home nonetheless, whether it's an airplane seat or a boarding house or an apartment.

Vicky and I hear the kids' giggling in their room as we retire to ours, finally horizontal after our long travel day, finally fully embarked on our journey.

Watering the Soul in the Riviera

IT'S NEXT MORNING—late morning, since we're still adjusting to the new time zone— and we're almost ready to hit the streets. Last item to pack: water bottles. Can't go out into the Riviera summer sun without our water bottles. Nietzsche writes in *Ecce Homo*, "I prefer towns in which opportunities abound for dipping from running wells (Nizza, Turin, Sils); a small glass accompanies me like a dog."[65] We don't anticipate being able to dip from running wells, so we take our water bottles, but the attention to hydration as the key to health is the same. One of the things I'm grateful to my wife for is convincing me to drink a tall glass of water with breakfast every morning—I used to have a daily mid-morning slump, but no more thanks to good hydration.

And this too is a Nietzschean lesson—we often attribute our moods and general performance to soul- or idea-related causes, but in fact most often the causes are physiological. I used to blame myself for those slumps or fall into a depressed way of thinking about things believing that I was accurately noticing the real nature of those things. In fact, it was only my own lack of hydration bringing me down. Here's how Nietzsche puts the matter in *Zarathustra*, with typical concision and accuracy:

---

65   EH clever.1

'Body am I, and soul'—thus speaks the
child. And why should one not speak like
children? But the awakened and knowing
say: body am I entirely, and nothing else; and
soul is only a word for something about the
body.

It's still okay to use soul-based vocabulary—for example,
I can talk about feeling down rather than being under-
hydrated. But I have to realize that when I say "I'm feeling
down" I'm describing something about my body, and so a
bodily solution—drinking a tall glass of water, e.g.—could
well be the answer, and I wind up feeling differently in my
soul as a result. It can work the other way, too—something
depresses me emotionally and I wind up with negative bodily
symptoms. But the interchangeability of bodily language and
soul-based language is one of Nietzsche's most important
principles. The soul is not some mysterious, ghostly entity
that floats in the air just above our heads, or a wraith-like gas
that exists in the interstices of our brains; rather it is a way of
describing our vital functions that proves quite useful so long
as we remember that the soul is not some separate entity, but
rather an aspect of our holistic selves.

ONCE the water bottles are filled, we still have to assemble
the guide sheets we printed off the Internet, find our cameras,
find our hats and load our various backpacks and camera bags.
At last—at last!—we're out the door. We walk back down
Rue de Gubernatis, across Avenue Felix Fauré and Boulevard
Jean Jaurès—the park in between them full of flowering trees,

magnificent in the sun—down the stairs of the Descente Crotti, and into the *vieille ville* of Nice.

If stepping onto the tram yesterday was stepping into the future, descending these stairs today is stepping into the past. It's about a decade per step, I'd say—by the bottom, we've reverted a couple of centuries. The stairs turn into a narrow street, which connects with other narrow streets joined together in a haphazard conglomeration. Most of the traffic is pedestrian, although there's an occasional vehicle, usually an electric cart or small truck making a delivery. Stone buildings crowd the street, a few painted in bright colors. Many have window boxes trailing flowers and all feature the same deteriorating, utterly charming shutters I noticed last night.

The streets are laid out haphazardly, as need dictated over the centuries, rather than by rational plan. In America, most cities have some sort of grid-like street pattern, so that if you start out on a street going north, you can continue in that direction for a good long time. In these old European cities, the streets follow ancient footpaths and cart paths. Maybe you had to avoid the root of a tree, now long gone, but remembered by a kink in a street, and the time-shadow of its existence continues to exist in the structures that eventually overwhelmed it. Indeed, over the course of centuries every available space has come to be used, so that buildings crowd against each other. The result is a maze-like construction that's oddly uniform even though it has resulted from untold years of natural growth. Stepping into these old cities is a matter of literally, physically entering into their history.

It's a world on a very human scale. The buildings, for example, are all three, four, or five stories tall because those were the limitations of the available building materials, not to mention the number of stairs people can tolerate in a building without an elevator. The streets are crooked because footpaths don't ever get worn in perfectly straight lines. The shops are small and open right onto the street. The city is built of stone but feels like an organism, one which has grown in symbiosis with its human residents.

I guide us through the narrow streets towards Cours Saleya. I'm the family navigator, a map-hound from earliest childhood. There's really nothing I enjoy more than navigating in a new place, or even in a familiar place but from a new angle. But I have to say I get a special thrill from navigating through the rich intricacy of old cities such as Nice. In American cities, you can navigate by directions—having gone north, you can now turn ninety degrees east, then ninety degrees south, and so on—but in an old city environment you can navigate only from the specific knowledge that this street empties into that one, this alley connects with that staircase, etc. An old city is personalized, individual, a world all its own.

The street signs in Vieux Nice are sunk right into the sides of buildings, in between the first and second stories. This contributes to the sense of the *vieille ville* as an organic construction. In modern American cities, streets are labeled by signs, as if someone passing through merely planted the sign and drove off. In old cities such as this, the street declares its own name in its own voice via the buildings which constitute it. It's as if the buildings and street have grown together as one organism, and now this organism is showing the passersby its own name tattooed into its very flesh.

All the streets in *vieux* Nice have double names, in two different languages: French and something which I had expected to be Italian but actually turns out to be an idiosyncratic dialect called Niçard. Niçard has some echoes of both French and Italian. For example, the French word *place* becomes *piazza* in Italian; the Niçard word for the same thing is *plassa*, a sort of hybrid.

The differences between the double street names in Nice are sometimes minor, as when *rue* is replaced with *carriera*, or *descente* with *calada*, and the rest of the name is the same or at least a close translation. Thus, Rue Droite is also Carriera Drecha, and Rue du Marché is also Carriera dóu Mercat. Other times, though, the street has an entirely different name in Niçard. For example, Rue Louis Gassin is also Carriera dóu Cours, and Rue Alexandre Mari is also Carriera dóu Pouònt-Nóu.

The reason for Nice having two home languages is that, though we think of Nice nowadays as a French city, in fact for most of its history Nice has been Nizza. Though now and again subjugated by French-speaking rulers from Provence—and occasionally pillaged by Muslim Saracens and Ottomans— the city long considered itself part of the Italian-speaking world and in 1388 formally placed itself under the protection of the House of Savoy. This royal family—whose palace we'll visit when we're in Turin—at times ruled a large area in what is now northwestern Italy and southeastern France, and at a certain point became rulers of Sicily as well. During the nineteenth-century *Risorgimento*[66], when Italy was moving towards becoming a unified, independent country, the House of Savoy made a deal in which it traded Nice and the surrounding area to France in exchange for France giving up its claims to other territories in northern Italy and supporting the unification of Italy under the Savoy ruler, Victor Emmanuel II. However, it was agreed that this territory swap could not take place without the consent of the locals and in 1860 a referendum was held. The vote was overwhelmingly in favor of the transfer—five centuries after submitting itself to the House of Savoy, the city at this point wanted to be

---

66   Literally "resurgence" or "revival," this is the term used for the process of Italian national reunification.

French. However, the vote was not unanimous, and Giuseppe Garibaldi, the famous Italian nationalist—who had himself been born in Nizza in 1807—took this to mean that the legal conditions of the transfer, which required "universal consent" of the inhabitants, had not in fact been met, and so, despite the vote, he tried to keep the city Italian. His local supporters, the Garibaldini as they called themselves, rioted frequently against the transfer throughout the 1860's. Though they had to be violently subdued, and despite their leader's rebelliousness against the new order, there is nonetheless a Place Garibaldi just outside the northern edge of the *vieille ville*. The city has been French ever since, except for a few years during World War II when, after the Germans had broken French power in the blitzkrieg of 1940, their Italian allies were able to rule the area again briefly.

It should be no surprise then that the Italian heritage in Nice is huge. Not only are all the street names doubled, but many of the official French street names are in fact adopted or adapted from Italian ones. Thus we came to Rue Alexandre Mari from Rue Raoul Bosio, after having arrived there from the Descente Crotti. Not only street and place names but also the art, architecture and especially the cuisine of Nice reflect Italian influence. It's part of what gives the place such charm—it's truly international, with direct ties to the histories of both Italy and France, with strong, long-standing tourist presences from both the English and the Russians (there is a Russian Orthodox church in the newer part of Nice, the Cathédrale St. Nicolas, which is one of the usual tourist high points), and more recent tourist populations of Germans and Americans (thus the street we'll cross to get from the Cours Saleya to the sea is Quai des États-Unis).

No wonder Nietzsche felt comfortable here. In *Human, All-Too-Human,* he had written that Europe was leaving the age of "self-enclosed original national cultures" and entering an "age of comparison... a time in which various different philosophies of life, customs, [and] cultures can be compared and experienced side by side."[67] He hadn't known it then, since he didn't arrive here until 1883, but he had just described Nice perfectly. During his time here, even though official administration had become French, the Italian feel of the place would still have been quite strong, likewise the idiosyncratic Niçard language, cuisine, and culture. Indeed, to his correspondents Nietzsche often identified his location as Nizza despite the transfer to France having taken place more than two decades earlier. In its intermingling of cultures and peoples, Nice/Nizza presented to Nietzsche the fulfillment of his prophecy:

> Trade and industry, the post and the book-trade, the possession in common of all higher culture, rapid changing of home and scene, the nomadic life now lived by all who do not own land—these circumstances are necessarily bringing with them a weakening and finally an abolition of nations ... so that as a consequence of continual crossing a mixed race, that of European man, must come into being out of them. This goal is at present being worked against ... by the separation of nations through the production of national hostilities.... It is not the interests of the many (the peoples) ... but above all the interests of certain princely dynasties and of certain classes of business and society that impel to this nationalism; once one has recognized this fact, one should

> not be afraid to proclaim oneself simply a
> *good European* and actively to work for the
> amalgamation of nations....[68]

After inventing the ideal of the "good European" in this passage from *Human, All-Too-Human* back in 1877, and then discovering Nice in 1883, Nietzsche employed the term again in 1885 in *Beyond Good and Evil*. However, its meaning has now shifted significantly. The "amalgamation of nations" wording from 1877 sounds like the erstwhile American ideal of the melting pot—a variety of cultures losing their distinctiveness and merging into one. But in *Beyond Good and Evil*, written after Nietzsche had spent a couple of seasons in Nice, good Europeans are now described as

> "those rarer and rarely contented human
> beings who are too comprehensive to find
> satisfaction in any fatherland and know how
> to love the south in the north and the north
> in the south."[69]

In this revised vision, south and north retain their identities, and the good Europeans are those who can appreciate divergent cultures.

It appears, then, that the experience of living in Nice changed Nietzsche's understanding of the good European.[70] Nice is a place that has been traded back and forth between different political powers, which has had conquerors from

---

68   HAH 475
69   BGE 254
70   To be sure, there are other things going on in Nietzsche's intellectual development (how could there not be?) which also affect this change. In particular, Nietzsche's early theory of truth, in which there is just one truth, fits nicely with the idea of cultures merging into one, whereas the idea of cultures remaining distinct fits nicely with perspectivism, in which there are multiple versions of the truth which cannot be reduced to, or assimilated into, any one final version of the truth.

any number of different directions, which hosted people in Nietzsche's time from all over Europe, and now from all over the world, and yet one which retains its local idiosyncrasies along with linguistic, culinary, artistic and architectural influences from many different cultures. Nice is indeed the perfect place to be a good European in Nietzsche's second, richer sense; Nice, and not Brussels, should really be today's European capital.

Living Nietzschean in Old Nice

DELIGHTING in the mix of people, the charming small shops, and the irrepressible sunshine which bursts upon us as we round corners and enter open spaces, we happily make our way through the *vieille ville*. Suddenly the narrow street opens into a wide *plassa*. On our left is an elegant former Savoy *palazzo* which is now the Palais de Justice. Ahead is a lovely church, the Chapelle de la Miséricorde, and across the way is our destination, Cours Saleya, an open-air market. [71]

The market itself is composed of a long string of vendor stands with aisles on either side. Everything is for sale: cheeses and wines and fruits and vegetables and spices and soaps and hats and souvenirs and breads and pastries, all the exhilarating bounty of Provençal agriculture, baking, and craft-making. The Cours is crowded with shoppers circling the vendors and with people walking to and from the beach, which is just outside the city wall along the Cours' southern side. At one end of the Cours is the Marché des Fleurs, where the flower-sellers cluster; at the other end is the Place Charles-Felix, a.k.a. the Plassa Carlou-Felis (we will later learn, when we visit his ancestral home outside of Turin, that Charles, or Carlou, was an important Savoy crown prince). In the low-slung buildings around the Cours are more shops, as well as restaurants preparing for lunchtime, with elegantly set

---

71   Note in these three sentences the successive appropriateness of French, Niçard, and Italian terms. I'm trying hard to be a good European!

tables extending out into the plaza and signboards advertising *specialitès de la maison.*

Outdoor markets are an entirely different experience from indoor ones. Buying our breakfast supplies last night in Galeries Lafayette, we had the pick of a phenomenal array of goods. But we chose on our own, in private, before emerging at the check-out line to submit our selections to the cashier's inspection. In an outdoor market, buying something is a human interaction. The vendor is right there across from you. He or she can see you, size you up, see what goods you're tempted by and what you're passing over, have a conversation, sometimes even offer you a taste. The impact of your buying or not buying is palpable and immediate for the vendor. Unlike in the department store, in an outdoor market, a sale is a memorable human interaction.

It's a savory one as well. Unlike in a modern supermarket, where everything is wrapped up, in the Cours Saleya everything is open to the air. As we circulate we catch delicate whiffs from the cheese vendors, powerful stenches from the fishmongers, and inspiring, ecstatic aromas from the spice vendors (after all, where did you think *herbes de provence* came from?). An outdoor market is also full of photographic possibilities, in which my kids revel. Sam's eye is primarily for interesting people; Rosie seeks out eye-catching arrays of spices, fruits and soaps; Eli's looking for interesting angles of the rows of awnings. Sam finds a staircase in one of the low-lying buildings on the south side of the Cours that emerges onto the building's roof, allowing a long perspective of the market. The rest of us climb up to join him. After admiring the bustle from up above, we turn around to get our first view since the airplane of the bright blue Mediterranean, sparkling in the sun.

When we return down the stairs, the market furnishes

us a superb picnic. I'm an olive fanatic and pick out three intriguing Niçoise varieties, Vicky locates tomatoes and cucumbers, Sam selects several exotic cheeses, Rosie finds fresh figs, Eli pulls out a couple of lengthy baguettes, and Miriam chooses some brilliant red raspberries. Then we exit the market to the south and cross Quai des États-Unis to the beachfront. Looking for shade, we wander eastward and wind up next to a big group of boulders tucked under a bend in the road. Above the road is a row of nineteenth century residences over which the cliff-front of the Colline du Chateau looms; before us runs the long stretch of beaches and hotels along the Promenade des Anglais off to the west, as far as the eye can see, and dominating the entire scene—the brilliant sea.

Krell entitles his chapter on Nietzsche's sojourns on the Riviera, "Intimate converse with the sea," citing Nietzsche's use of this phrase in his autobiography to describe the origins of his book *Daybreak*.[72] For a man with few friends, most experiences of the sea would have been solitary, with the continuous crash of the waves the only sound to match the continuous crash of his thoughts. In my case, my close encounter with the Mediterranean includes the burbles and exclamations of my family enjoying the marvelous food we've bought. The fresh figs in particular are a revelation—and you know what? Our hero even had something to say about figs, in the mouth of Zarathustra:

> The figs are falling from the trees; they are good and sweet; and, as they fall, their red skin bursts. I am a north wind to ripe figs. Thus, like figs, these teachings fall to you, my friends; now consume their juice and their sweet meat.[73]

72   EH books.D.1 (Kaufmann translates this phrase as "secrets with the sea".)
73   Z II.2, repeated in EH Preface.4

A philosophy as sweet as fresh figs—that's a fine philosophy indeed.

When our picnic is through, we re-gird ourselves with our backpacks and our camera bag. Well-fortified with Provençal cheese and fresh figs, we are now ready for our business of the day: to find Nietzsche's residences in Nice.

Well, two of Nietzsche's residences. He lived in four different places in Nice over the five winters he spent here, sometimes switching mid-winter in search of more space or better light or to save a few francs.

The first was on Rue Cathérine Ségurane, on the far, eastern side of the Parc du Chateau. The *parc* includes a huge hill, the Colline du Chateau, which functions as a sort of boundary wall at the eastern end of the *vielle ville*. This residence is thus not an especially convenient location for us to get to; we will content ourselves with zooming past it on the bus to Èzé tomorrow.

The second residence, and the one he returned to most frequently, was the Pension de Genève on the *petite* Rue St. Etienne. Isn't that a lovely name for a street? I picture a little alley or mews and a house dripping with flower boxes. However, all I can do is picture it: the entire street was razed many years ago so that the railway station could be expanded.

Instead, our first goal for today is to find Nietzsche's last residence in Nice. That is, it was the last of the four he discovered. His actual last winter in Nice in 1888 was spent back at the Pension de Genève, on the first floor of the building whose fourth floor had been damaged in the earthquake of 1887. I'm a bit puzzled as to why he would trust even the first floor of a building whose fourth floor had been rendered uninhabitable by an earthquake. But then again, one of his most famous passages urges us to live dangerously:

> [T]he secret of the greatest fruitfulness
> and the greatest enjoyment of existence is:
> to live dangerously! Build your cities under
> Vesuvius! Send your ships into uncharted
> seas![74]

I have always thought he means this metaphorically and intellectually; that is, he isn't recommending that we cross the street without looking, but rather that we break away from old, comfortable ways of thought and living and try out new, risky ideas. But when I think about him returning to Nice the year after the earthquake and living on a lower floor of a building whose upper floor was damaged in that earthquake, I wonder if maybe he meant it literally. (It's likely the rent that year was really low.) Perhaps he means that a brush with danger provides a *frisson* that helps us appreciate and enjoy life and urges us to reject the safety of the modern developed world in order to feel that again. One thing's for sure: he definitely enjoyed himself in the aftermath of the earthquake, as he wrote in a letter the next day:

> Nizza has just had its lengthy
> international carnival ... and, immediately
> after that, six hours after its last *girandola*
> [JC—a rotating firework], new and more
> seldom tasted delights of life arrived.
> We are living, in fact, in the interesting
> expectation *that we shall perish*—thanks
> to a well-intentioned earthquake, which is
> making the dogs howl far and wide, and
> not only the dogs. What fun, when the old
> houses rattle overhead like coffee mills!
> when the ink bottle assumes a life of its

own! when the streets fill with half-dressed
figures and shattered nervous systems!
Last night between two and three o'clock,
comme gaillard as I am [JC—this phrase
is somewhat untranslatable—N seems
to mean he was playing the part of a jolly
fellow], I toured the various districts of the
town to see where the fear is greatest. The
population is camping out day and night—
it looked nice and military. And now even
in the hotels!—where there has been much
damage and so complete panic prevails.
I found all my friends, men and women,
stretched out miserably under green trees,
heavily flannelled, for it was bitterly cold,
and thinking dark thoughts of the end every
time a small shock came. I have no doubt
that this will bring the *saison* to a sudden
end—everyone is thinking of *leaving*....
Already yesterday evening the guests at the
hotel where I eat could not be persuaded
to take their *table d'hôte* indoors—people
ate and drank outside; and except for an
old, very pious lady, who is convinced that
the good Lord is not entitled to do her any
harm, I was the only cheerful person in a
crowd of masks and 'feeling hearts.'[75]

An earthquake with everyone expecting to die—what fun!
Is this just a brave face he's putting on? The letter ends with
a P.S. apologizing for shaky handwriting; Nietzsche says he
had to hurry to get the letter onto the next train, but was
he possibly more spooked than he lets on? He is certainly
reveling in *schadenfreude* (to use another untranslatable phrase

---

75   Letter to Reinhart von Seydlitz, February 24, 1887 = Middleton #150

from another language) at the sight of all the hoity-toity turned out onto the sidewalks in the middle of the night. But here too one has to wonder at his real emotions. After all, when the fuss was over, it was they and not he who re-entered those hotels, where he could afford to eat once a day but not take a room. One last thought: The analogy Nietzsche draws between his own cheerfulness and the secure faith of the pious old lady reflects his idea that his new, godless way of thinking will satisfactorily replace traditional monotheism by providing a similar sense of peace with whatever transpires.[76] The old lady has faith that, whatever random disaster occurs, there is an intelligence up above which ensures that all is as it should be. Nietzsche, on the other hand, holds that the world is utterly random and that the proper attitude to take is to revel in its randomness and to love one's fate anyway. And in this remarkable letter, he is walking the walk, or I guess the most I can say is that he's talking the walk.

In a different letter about the earthquake, Nietzsche counts the destruction of the fourth floor of the Pension de Genève as a "positive side" of the earthquake, in that now posterity will have one less "pilgrimage site" to visit.[77] In our case, at least, that's entirely true, and so today we seek not the Pension de Genève but instead the place Nietzsche was living in at the time of the earthquake, the spot where he wrote these letters, 29 Rue de Ponchettes.

Rue de Ponchettes runs parallel to the Cours Saleya on its southern side; thus the row of buildings forming the southern side of the Cours, atop which we stood to get our panoramic view before acquiring our picnic, is the same row of buildings that forms the northern side of Rue de Ponchettes. The buildings' southern exposure was precisely the appeal this

76 See HAH 107
77 Letter to Emily Fynn, in Krell & Bates 193 fn 5

residence had for Nietzsche. You see, the French Riviera is generally considered a warm place, and of course our visit here comes during the summer, but it is still Europe and winter can be chilly. In his letters home from Nice, Nietzsche often regretted not having a stove, or, if he had one, bemoaned how poorly it worked; in several of these letters he apologizes for writing with "blue fingers."[78] So an affordable room with southern exposure was a find.

From its beginning at the eastern end of the Cours, Rue de Ponchettes runs further eastward all the way along the south side of the *vieille ville* to the foot of the Colline du Chateau. It's primarily a residential street and most of the houses are numbered, so we set out expecting it will be easy to find Nietzsche's residence. However, despite several traverses of the entire street I can't find a building numbered 29. The best guess I can make is a slightly discouraging one, namely that Nietzsche's former residence is now the storage area in the rear of a restaurant whose front opens onto the Cours Saleya.

Oh well, life goes on. One of Nietzsche's teachings is that "life operates *essentially*, that is, in its basic functions, through injury, assault, exploitation, destruction, and simply cannot be thought of at all without this character."[79] We commonly think of nature as a peaceful harmony, but in fact all ecosystems are composed of competing elements trying to eat each other, or overshadow each other, or uproot each other, or take each other's resources. Nature, in Nietzsche's interpretation, consists of "the tyrannically inconsiderate and relentless enforcement of claims of power"[80] and since a large part of his philosophical project is "to translate man back

---

78   Krell & Bates 193; see also letter to Peter Gast October 27, 1887 = Middleton #156
79   GM II.11
80   BGE 22

into nature,"[81] this would apply to the humanly constructed world as well. "If a temple is to be erected *a temple must be destroyed.*"[82] And so, likewise, if a restaurant needs a back room, or the railway station needs to expand, a former residence of Nietzsche's must be destroyed. I'm pretty sure the man himself would be good with it, and so I decide I will follow in his footsteps on this point.

There is another former residence in *vieux* Nice though, where Nietzsche lived during the winter of 1885-86. Since there is a photo of this one in *The Good European,* I have high hopes of finding it un-destroyed. We re-enter Cours Saleya and pursue our quarry out the other end, westward. After traversing the brilliantly colored and transportingly fragrant Marché des Fleurs, we head down Rue François de Paule. We come upon the Opera House, an impressive structure with statues of musical heroes worked into the ornate façade of the building. Nietzsche heard a performance of Bizet's *Carmen,* his all-time favorite opera, right here shortly after arriving. Then we pass more stores, including one large store devoted entirely to olive oil—hundreds of different varieties. These will arrive in America in a few years, but for now this is another Provençal wonder.

Finally, there it is: number 26, Rue François de Paule. Nietzsche lived on the *2e étage à gauche,* facing north, which was a mixed blessing—the indirect light was good for his eyes, but not so good for heating the room. The large, handsome building now apparently serves primarily as a source of offices for *avocats,* who are not avocados (as Eli playfully suggests) but lawyers (as Rosie patiently corrects him). It looks like a nice place to live, both the building itself and its location. Sitting at the western apex of the *vieille ville,* it is right across

---

81   BGE 230
82   GM II.24

from a little park, the Place des Phocéens, which is the western end of the series of parks along the *avenues* on either side of Place Massena. The other side of the building faces the sea. To the west is the graceful curve of the coast along the Bai des Anges, with all the elegant hotels in a row. Back behind us lie the Opera House, the Cours Saleya and the rest of the *vielle ville*. A nice place to live. We finish our picnic in the Place des Phocéens.

And later we have dinner at a kosher restaurant in the newer part of the city. In retrospect, it might have made more sense to find a more idiosyncratically Niçoise establishment, but kosher restaurants are a rare treat for us, so we go for it. The food is still exotic, since the place is run by French Jews with some connection to France's former North African colonies, Morocco and Algeria. Sam and Rosie try out their French on the waitress. They initially struggle and I begin trying to help, but Vicky touches my arm; "Let them," she whispers. And eventually Sam and Rosie successfully order us several different couscous *tajins*. The food is only so-so, but the desserts are good. We return the same way we set out, by way of Rue Massena, which connects with Place Massena to the northwest and is a pedestrians-only street featuring shops, food, and street performers.

We pass through Place Massena and find that the bizarre white figures atop poles are lit up from the inside in a variety of jewel colors. Full of good couscous and the magic of Nice, we collapse into our beds more than satisfied with our first day, ready for the big event tomorrow—Èzé, and the path that Friedrich Nietzsche made his own.

The Eternal Recurrence of Èzé

During his first winter in Nice, Nietzsche took a day trip to Èzé, a medieval, walled village a few miles to the east that has survived the centuries virtually unchanged. Even at the time this was a common tourist destination. It involved taking the train along the coast to a spot known, reasonably enough, as Èzé la Gare (*gare* means station). After getting off the train, the other tourists rode in a carriage up to the top of the mountain, where the medieval village is. Nietzsche, however, spurned the carriage and hiked up a steep path to get there. Along the way, he composed what became the "On Old and New Tablets" section of the third part of *Thus Spoke Zarathustra*, including the following passage:

> 'Why so hard?' the kitchen coal once said to the diamond. 'After all, are we not close kin?'
>
> Why so soft? O my brothers, thus I ask you: are you not after all my brothers?
>
> Why so soft, so pliant and yielding? Why is there so much denial, self-denial, in your hearts? So little destiny in your eyes?
>
> And if you do not want to be destinies and inexorable ones, how can you triumph

with me?

And if your hardness does not wish to flash and cut and cut through, how can you one day create with me?

For creators are hard. And it must seem blessedness to you to impress your hand on millennia as on wax.

Blessedness to write on the will of millennia as on bronze—harder than bronze, nobler than bronze. Only the noblest is altogether hard.

This new tablet, O my brothers, I place over you: *become hard!*[83]

The passage is powerful on its own, but it takes on a striking, down-to-earth backlight once you know the story. Softness and hardness are standing in not only for big concepts such as pity versus "tough love" (a frequent Nietzschean theme, although he doesn't use the phrase "tough love," of course) but also for more mundane things such as climbing up a mountain rather than taking the carriage. The other tourists took the soft way; Nietzsche took the hard way and he clearly feels he's the better person for it. Rising to the challenge activates his toughness and prepares him to be a noble creator.

Krell, in his introduction to *The Good European*, warns against reductively connecting Nietzsche's work sites to the work produced there. You shouldn't assume, according to Krell, that the particular locale is what gave Nietzsche the particular idea:

[W]hat are we to make of it when Nietzsche tells us that he conceived the "Old and New Tablets" episode of *Thus Spoke*

Zarathustra while climbing the path at Èzé, near Nice, or that the thought of eternal return overwhelmed him near a pyramidal boulder at Surlej? "Of Old and New Tablets" is a long and carefully composed text: it was not written on a hike....

To push the question harder: Can one calculate the influence of Nietzsche's work sites on his principal ideas...? Is eternal return a thought of Alpine lakes, will to power an effulgence of the northern Italian city-states, overman a dream of the mountains near Nice, genealogy a strategy for defeating the tourists at Sils-Maria? Such judgments could only be quirky, and this book has no desire to make them.[84]

At a certain level Krell has an irrefutable point: Nietzsche cannot expect his readers to know where and how his writing was produced (unless he gives specific information about it, which he doesn't in the case of "On Old and New Tablets"), so his writing must convey its ideas on its own, without help from photos of the site where it was conceived or descriptions of the conditions under which it was produced. It's also true that a place does not determine the thought produced in it; otherwise all those who had ever walked past that boulder would also have had the same thought of the eternal return.

All the same, Professor Krell, I beg to differ. For one thing, Nietzsche could well have written the entire "Old and New Tablets" passage on that hike. He could surely have stopped on his way up the mountain (and down again, later) to record his reflections in the notebook he always carried, and as we'll see the hike takes a good hour or more, so there's plenty

---

84   Krell & Bates 5-6 (but compare 154)

of time for a substantial passage. Of course, he revised and
polished it later at his writing desk and revised it again when
preparing the full manuscript for the publisher. But I don't
see why the first draft couldn't have been written on foot.

And for another thing, I don't mind being quirky—it's
a perfectly appropriate Nietzschean individual thing to be,
after all—and in this book I have every desire to connect
Nietzsche's ideas with the places and times they were produced.
At the very least, one can gain a better understanding of
some of Nietzsche's ideas from knowledge of the sites of their
production; one can get a better sense of what he's talking
about. We already noted in the last chapter, how living in
Nice not only reflected but actually seems to have changed
Nietzsche's own understanding of what it means to be "a
good European." We in our turn, having been to the places
where these ideas meant something in Nietzsche's life, will
be better equipped when we return to our own locations, to
figure out what meaning these ideas might have in *our* lives.
So knowing the location can be helpful. Krell is being a
careful scholar when he states that one can't assume anything
while considering the relation between Nietzsche's ideas and
his work sites.   Here in this book, however, we are trying
to figure out what Nietzsche's ideas might mean in practical
terms. How could they influence our lives? How *should* they
influence our lives?

"Become hard," for example—what could that mean in
practical terms? Well, pertaining to the situation in which
Nietzsche first thought of the idea, it might mean walking
instead of riding. That might sound like a trivial bit of
advice, but it will be beneficial for one's health and for the
environment, and it's not hard to imagine that a habitual
rider who became a habitual walker would thereby have a
changed life.

More generally, and more instructively, the injunction to "become hard" can be extended to our values, our opinions, our life choices. Rather than take the easy path and follow the crowd, we can push ourselves to live as Nietzschean individuals. Living in the early years of mass society, Nietzsche sees European culture tending towards stagnant conformism and the triumph of "the last man," craven and small-minded, who does nothing but play it safe.[85] He thinks the key to healthy culture is for free spirits to go their own way and develop new ideas so that culture can develop in new ways as well. Doing so might be hard, but the benefits, as I've noted above, will accrue to both the culture and the individual.

"Become hard" means, finally, embracing what's difficult instead of taking it easy. Modernity seems to consist of nothing but devices and institutional structures that will make life easier—but does that make life meaningful? Perhaps it is the difficulties we undertake that do that. There's a terrific passage in Kierkegaard where he describes sitting in a café as a young man, trying to decide what to do with his life. He observes people in the street before him rushing hither and thither, working hard to try to make life easier—by making better machines, producing more wealth and so on—but Kierkegaard decides, "out of the same humanitarian impulse," as he says, "to spread difficulties everywhere."[86] I think Nietzsche had exactly the same thing in mind. An easier life is not necessarily a better life. It is the hard things we do, the obstacles we overcome, that make our lives meaningful and make us proud to be human.

And it is precisely an instance of hiking instead of riding that might provoke all these thoughts in Nietzsche and crystallize his philosophy. In turn, a reader might get the

---

85   Z Prologue.5
86   *Concluding Unscientific Postscript*, 185

point precisely by reflecting on this sort of experience. As a consequence, that same reader might in turn make it a habit to seek out harder things and as a result, have a changed life. If philosophy is to matter in our lives, if Nietzsche is to be a teacher, such connections must be thought through.

There's a broader point here, one which goes to the heart of this book. My graduate advisor, Alexander Nehamas, says that Nietzsche's biography is of interest for its own sake, but should be kept separate from his philosophy. Nietzsche's readers would not have known his personal story, so his philosophy must be able to stand on its own merits. Nietzsche must convince us of his philosophical points directly, without appeal to his life circumstances (which would commit the fallacy of special pleading at least, and perhaps *ad hominem* and appeal to pity as well).

To a certain extent this principle is well-taken. Nietzsche owes us philosophical reasons, not biographical ones, for his changes in view. He can't say, "Well, I'm no longer friends with Wagner, and that's why I'm writing against everything I wrote before." He owes us reasons why *we* should turn against Wagner, we who have never been friends with the composer.

However, Nietzsche also writes that he learns not just from what philosophers say, but how they live. And his own philosophy is one which emphasizes the lived significance of ideas—both where ideas come from and what practical import they have. "The only critique of a philosophy ... that proves something [is] trying to see whether one can live in accordance with it."[87] We are thus in fact following in Nietzsche's footsteps quite closely when we turn this thought onto Nietzsche himself. Where and how did Nietzsche live? How did it affect his thinking? Nietzsche addresses these questions in his autobiography, from which we have heard

---

87   UM III.8

and will be hearing now and again in these pages. But we would surely be mistaken to take him solely at his own word. We will gain perspective on what he says by putting ourselves in his shoes—or at least, on his walking paths—and so come to understand him better. Returning then to our own paths, we will understand better how we are different.

IT was Nietzsche's famous walk in Èzé that inspired me to propose it for our itinerary. We planned it for our second full day in Nice, with the idea that we'd make the first day an easy one to get over the rigors of travel and adjust for jet lag, and still have the third day in reserve in case something went wrong on the second day, which it almost did.

During my pre-trip navigational research, however, I found an added element I had not previously known, namely that there is a path named for Nietzsche in Èzé—the Chemin Friedrich Nietzsche. It connects with the main drag in the medieval village, the Avenue du Jardin Exotique, and then runs all the way down the hill to the train station. So the footpath between the train station and the medieval village of Èzé has by now become so identified with Nietzsche that the village of Èzé has officially named the path after him. And if you're calling your family vacation to Europe "In Nietzsche's Footsteps," then well, you've got to hike this path.

Once we were actually in Nice though, we decided we didn't have to do everything just as he did. He took the train, but our apartment is closer to the bus station and the bus is cheaper. More importantly, since we were a bit worried about the heat and how our younger members might fare hiking up what we assumed was a steep and difficult path, and since we didn't want everyone to be worn out when we reached the medieval village, we decided we would take the bus to the top, explore the medieval village first, and then hike down to the train station.

It's a little past twelve when we reach the Gare Routière. We ask a transit worker which bus to take for Èzé and he tells us to take the *quatre-vingt-deux*. However, it turns out we have just missed the 82. We could wait for another, but there won't be another for an hour and forty-five minutes, and having gotten out of the apartment so late, we don't really want to delay even more.

So we look around at the other schedules posted on the walls. There's another stop listed on the bus 100 schedule, a couple stops after Èzé la Gare, called Èzé Gianton. Èzé, as I understood from the Nietzsche story and from my map work, is a two-level place: *la gare* is at the bottom of the hill, by the sea (in fact, the very next stop on the 100 line after *la gare* is called Saint-Laurent-d'Èzé Plage—*plage* is the word for beach), and then the medieval village is at the top of the hill. So if the bus goes past *la gare* and *la plage* and comes to Èzé Gianton, that means it turns up the hill and goes to Èzé le Village or at least close. Èzé Gianton must be close to Èzé le Village—how big could the place be?

Well, pretty big as it turns out. In 2008, roughly 125 years after Nietzsche climbed from its train station to its ancient castle-top, Èzé has become a sprawling place, spread over several hills, stretching a long way along the coast, as well as a good way up into the surrounding mountains. Èzé Gianton is basically on the way out of town towards Monaco. It's only part way up the hill, nowhere near the top and nowhere near the medieval village.

It is, however, incontrovertibly and undeniably where we are when I realize my mistake. We ask to get off and ask the driver what bus we can take to get from here up to *le village*.

He suggests the 83, which provides local service within Èzé. We get off the bus feeling hopeful. But when we look at the schedule for the 83, we find that it runs every hour for most of the day but takes an hour-and-forty-five-minute break in the middle of the day. We are just about at the beginning of that long break, meaning we now face about a 90-minute wait in the heat, in the middle of nowhere.

I spend the entire hour and a half kicking myself. The family counts on me to be the navigator and the public transportation expert. And here I have managed to get us stuck for an hour and a half on a remote hillside in the middle of nowhere in the blazing midday sun with time ticking away on our one precious day to explore Èzé.

And not only that—I now have an eternal recurrence problem. It's a lot to explain, but don't worry, we have time.

THE IDEA of the eternal recurrence goes back at least to the ancient Stoics, possibly back even further to Heraclitus. But Nietzsche made such a big deal of it, he essentially made it his own. Here's the passage in which he introduces it:

> *The greatest weight* – What if some day or night a demon were to steal after you into your loneliest loneliness and say to you: 'This life as you now live it and have lived it, you will have to live once more and innumerable times more; and there will be nothing new in it, but every pain and every joy and every thought and sigh and everything unutterably small or great in your life will have to return to you, all in the same succession

and sequence—even this spider and this moonlight between the trees, and even this moment and I myself. The eternal hourglass of existence is turned upside down again and again, and you with it, speck of dust!'[88]

In his later notebooks—the ones published by his sister after his breakdown, despite his instructions that they be burned—Nietzsche attempted several scientific proofs of the eternal recurrence. For example, if the number of particles in the world is finite and time is infinite, eventually the arrangement of those particles must be repeated and in fact, repeated an infinite number of times.[89] It's sort of like saying that a deck of cards, shuffled enough times, will inevitably return to its original arrangement. However, reading what Nietzsche actually *published* about the recurrence—namely the passage above and some similar passages in *Zarathustra*— he never attempts a serious proof. The question is what *effect* the thought of recurrence has on you, and what it would mean for you to *believe* it to be true.

Of course, even if we understand the recurrence psychologically, it is possible to be skeptical. If in fact everything repeats itself exactly the same way, including the fact that I don't have foreknowledge of what will happen, then the recurrence of my life need have no effect on me whatsoever. That is, since continual *déjà vu* is not a feature of my current life, it wouldn't be a feature of my future lives either. I would simply live my life all over again, just as oblivious as the "first" time and so on and on into eternity. And thus, the thought of the recurrence need have no effect on me at all.

---

88   GS 341
89   See, for example, section 1066 in the selection of notebook passages published by Elisabeth under the title *The Will to Power*

Nietzsche however, thinks there are only two possible reactions to being confronted with the thought of recurrence. Here's how he continues the quote from above:

> Would you not throw yourself down and gnash your teeth and curse the demon who spoke thus? Or have you once experienced a tremendous moment when you would have answered him: 'You are a god and never have I heard anything more divine.' If this thought gained possession of you, it would change you as you are or perhaps crush you. The question in each and every thing, 'Do you desire this once more and innumerable times more?' would lie upon your actions as the greatest weight. Or how well-disposed would you have to become to yourself and to life *to crave nothing more fervently* than this ultimate eternal confirmation and seal?

If I regretted some event in my life and then was told that I'd have to relive it over and over and over, it would make the thought of that event horribly oppressive. I'd be unable to say, "Well, it was just that one time" and then just look to the future, because, thanks to the recurrence, my future actually includes my past too.[90] Or if I were in the midst of something unpleasant right now, I wouldn't be able to console myself, "This too shall pass," and just hunker down till it's over, because, thanks to the recurrence, it will continually come back around. So one of the things Nietzsche is trying to accomplish with this idea is to block you from saying that this life is a vale of tears but that's okay since this suffering

---

90 For this reason, Nietzsche often says, in *Zarathustra* as well as his notebooks, that the recurrence turns time into a circle.

will be requited in an afterlife. Nietzsche says you can't get out of it so easily. Rather, you have to think that *this is it*, the only life you'll ever have, and if you judge it negatively, you're condemning yourself for all eternity.

Nietzsche, having been raised a good Christian, still thinks of eternity as the highest seal of approval, but what he's now attempting to do is place that value of eternity on each and every moment. What he wants you to do is love life—this life right here and now, in this very present moment—so much that you would affirm having it repeated into all eternity. For him this is the ultimate test of value—do you affirm your life the way it is? Is what you're doing now worthy of being repeated into all eternity? And to hit home the hardest: Do you affirm *yourself* just the way you are?

But the thought of recurrence is even heavier than that. I mentioned earlier Nietzsche's statement that "all things (are) knotted together so firmly..." that if you want to affirm one moment, you have to affirm them all. This makes affirmation incredibly difficult. In fact, I would argue it makes it impossible or at least indecent, since I would then have to say that any moment of joy for me is affirmable only if it was worth having the entire Holocaust happen.

The only way I can think of affirmation is to draw some sort of horizon. The image I have in mind is the way ripples move in a pond away from the point at which a rock splashes into it. If the pond is big enough, eventually the ripples will dissipate into still water. In the same way, I can't imagine my single happiness justifying the Holocaust, but I can imagine a moment of joy for me justifying many of the moments around it—e.g. the joy of eating supper justifies having to wash the dishes afterwards. In fact, it would be a measure of a moment's greatness the more other moments it could justify. Thus, meeting and marrying my wife justified a lot of earlier moments—all the heartbreaks of my pre-marriage romantic life were now justified because they were necessary for me to not be attached to anyone else and thus be able to meet and marry my wife. In this way I can accept the idea that affirming a moment requires affirming many other moments too, the ones with which it is knotted.

So the question for me, right here and now at the Èzé Gianton bus stop, waiting in the hot sun for that damn bus to come, is not whether I want to make the same mistake over and over and over again—of course, I don't. It's that I have to realize that the mistake is knotted together firmly with everything else that goes along with it. And while strict application of Nietzsche's idea would require that it's knotted together with everything from what I had for breakfast this morning to Caesar crossing the Rubicon, I'll hold it only to the "local" standard—can I will the recurrence of this mistake given everything that went on in the rest of this day, the rest of our day-trip to Èzé?

To evaluate that, I have to tell you how the Professional Travelers react to our predicament. And you know what? My family doesn't get down on me at all, God bless them. Not even a little bit.

There is a small kiosk across the road, in what looks like a park-and-ride for people commuting to work in Nice or Monaco, and we walk over and get sandwiches.

"They have tomato-basil-mozzarella panini! Yesssss!" Eli and Miriam, who have decided to count how many of these ubiquitous sandwiches they have on the trip, stick their arms in the air triumphantly, then high-five–this is their second one in two days.

"Tuna?" asks Sam. "*Avez-vous tuna?*"

The rest of us have *pan bagnat*, which is what a tuna sandwich is called in Nice. "It means literally 'wet bread,'"

Rosie explains. "*Pan* is like *pain*, the French word for bread—it's the Niçard equivalent—and *bagnat* is like *bain,* the French word for bath." *Pan bagnat* includes, besides the tuna, tomato and lettuce one customarily gets in a tuna sandwich in the States, exotic things like olives, hard-boiled eggs, and—a special treat for my particular taste buds—anchovies. It's basically a *salade niçoise* in sandwich form and believe me, it really works.

As we eat, Sam and Eli call out the make and model of the sports cars zipping by on their way to Monaco, while Rosie, Miriam, and Vicky look down into the gardens of the mansions arrayed on the hillside below us. Most of all, we gaze at the grand expanse of the Mediterranean, crisscrossed by occasional boats (including some fairly spectacular yachts), stretching in its fabulous blue glory to the distant horizon.

"Good spot for a picnic," says Vicky.

I will always be grateful that my family did not get angry with me for my goof, did not even so much as roll their eyes at me. Thanks, Professional Travelers.

But does this solve my eternal recurrence problem? Nietzsche requires not just that things be not as bad as possible, but that we find our lives worthy of being repeated into all eternity. His way of putting the point is to challenge us to consider each and every moment in this way. So, was this unexpected picnic at Èzé Gianton good enough that I would affirm its eternal recurrence? That is, can I say I would *choose* to screw up with the buses that same way again, over and over for all eternity?

Try as I might, I don't think I can. Maybe it's because my mistake caused the whole thing, so that as good as the picnic was, as heartwarming as it was that my family made the best of it, reliving the event would be to relive my mistake too and my pride can't take that. Besides, we were just making the best of it, not doing what we would have chosen to do above all else.

Maybe I can say that getting the bus routes wrong was necessary for me to learn how to do them right, so if the learning is the crucial thing, I actually did it just right and can affirm its recurrence. But no, turning the mistake into a learning moment so that now I can be the-teacher-of-how-to-get-to-Èzé—just as Zarathustra is the teacher of the overman and of the eternal recurrence—isn't working for me. It's not enough to get me to affirm the recurrence of my mistake. It would have been definitely better to have taken the right bus and gotten right to Èzé le Village. We'd have had more time in its winding streets, more time to shop and probably a better lunch than the one we got from the kiosk.

All right, so let's try again. Zarathustra teaches that "if you have an enemy, do not requite him evil with good.... Rather, prove that he did you some good."[91] That is, don't just endure your suffering, let alone turn the other cheek; rather, turn your suffering into a positive gain for yourself.

Nietzsche applies this principle to himself in some dramatic ways. For example, in *Ecce Homo* he describes how he wrote another book, *The Dawn*:[92]

> The following winter, my first one in Genoa, that sweetening and spiritualization which is almost inseparably connected with an extreme poverty of blood and muscle produced *The Dawn*. The perfect brightness and cheerfulness, even exuberance of the spirit, reflected in this work is compatible

---

91   Z I.19

92   The standard translation, by Hollingdale, renders the title as *Daybreak*; I'm using *The Dawn* here because that's what Kaufmann uses in the following quote from his translation of EH.

in my case not only with the most profound physiological weakness, but even with an excess of pain. In the midst of the torments that go with an uninterrupted three-day migraine, accompanied by laborious vomiting of phlegm, I possessed a dialectician's clarity *par excellence* and thought through with very cold blood matters for which under healthier circumstances I am not mountain-climber, not subtle, not *cold* enough.[93]

Now, you might expect him to say that it's a good book *in spite of* the migraine, but what he actually says is that it's a good book *because of* the migraine: since he could not concentrate for long, it was necessary for him to write very tersely and directly. The need to be brief, he claims, improved his style. That is, he *needed* the migraine in order to write as well as he did.

I wish I could also say that we *needed* to get on the wrong bus to have a good experience at Èzé, but, well, I can't really. This was an "in spite of," not a "because of."

Except here I am *writing* about it, hoping this account of our impromptu picnic at Èzé Gianton makes this a better book, good enough to get published, good enough to get people to read it, good enough to get people to enjoy it, good enough to get people to try Nietzsche, to try philosophy, to engage in its sweet intellectual inquiry and so enrich their lives. If we had just taken the right bus, we would have had a good time at Èzé, maybe a better time than we actually had, but I wouldn't have had as much to write about, wouldn't have had such a good opening to discuss the eternal recurrence. So, taking the wrong bus *was* in fact *necessary* for something good to happen—the writing of this chapter in the book.

93   EH wise.1

And this, I think, is ultimately the point of the eternal recurrence: It's not about simply evaluating the moments of one's life. If it were, some moments would inevitably not make the cut, since we are such fallible beings. No, I think the eternal recurrence is about the impetus to *justify* one's moments. If something bad happens, *make* it into something good. In this case, I'm turning my gaffe into a vehicle for teaching about one of the most perennially interesting aspects of Nietzsche's philosophy. The challenge of the recurrence is not to prove that we enjoyed ourselves in spite of the mistake, but rather to prove that the mistake did us some good.

So even though we can separate our moments of sorrow from our moments of joy, the thing we need to do, the essence of Nietzsche's teaching of the eternal recurrence, is not just to distinguish them from each other but to actively strive to turn the former into the latter. In this way, we change the past and so in a sense, fulfill the circular conception of time that the recurrence implies. And so, while I still kick myself about my bus mistake and though the calm, supportive reaction of the Professional Travelers was heart-warming and quite eternally affirmable, it's really the time and effort spent finding the positive effect of the event that matters in the end.

I'll try to hold on to that and I'll try to always affirm this particular moment eternally: the strange, unpredictable and unexpected joy of sitting with my wife and children in a plexiglass bus stop on a remote hillside on a fine summer's day in a little town near Nice, munching some unexpectedly excellent *pan bagnat*, car-spotting some swanky Porsches and Ferraris, peering into the verdant private gardens of Riviera mansions, and gazing at the indescribably brilliant, sublimely deep, endlessly forgiving blue of the sea.

The Nietzschean Hike

THE 83 FINALLY arrives. It's crowded, of course—after all, all across town people have been waiting an hour and forty-five minutes for this bus. My family has to stand in the aisle, and my spot is in the well, right by the thin plexiglass of the doors, with a close-up view of the pavement as it whooshes past. We sway patiently through the 180-degree switchbacks up the side of the mountain, and eventually we come to Èzé le Village. After a snack and a short stop at an outdoor market, where I acquire some lavender tea which I will savor for weeks after we return home, we stroll up the path to the walled city.

The existence of Èzé was first officially recorded in Roman times, but it is believed to have been originally settled by the Phoenicians around 2000 BCE. In fact, the temple they built to Isis may have given the place its name. Some may be wondering why the Phoenicians built a temple to an Egyptian goddess and all I can say (other than to remind you of the possibility that the story has gotten garbled over the centuries) is that pagan cultures often borrowed from each other. It's not until monotheism comes along that we see the phenomenon of one religion trying to squeeze out all competing religions. This live-and-let-live celebration of multicultural diversity is part of why Nietzsche celebrated paganism. He also believed the multiplicity of gods allowed people to be unique individuals:

> *The great advantage of polytheism.* —For an individual to posit his own ideal and to derive from it his own law, joys, and rights—that may well have been considered hitherto as the most outrageous human aberration.... The few who dared as much always felt the need to apologize to themselves, usually by saying: 'It wasn't I! Not I! But *a god* through me.' The wonderful art and gift of creating gods—polytheism—was the medium through which this impulse could discharge, purify, perfect, and ennoble itself....
>
> Monotheism, on the other hand, this rigid consequence of the doctrine of one normal human type—the faith in one normal god beside whom there are only pseudo-gods—was perhaps the greatest danger that has yet confronted humanity. It threatened us with the premature stagnation that, as far as we can see, most other species have long reached....[94]

In his later works he calls the belief in a single deity in whose image *all* of us were created "monotonotheism."[95] It's a wonderful coinage and there's surely a tendency in monotheistic faiths to think that the ideal human type has been defined, deviation from which is not only immoral but blasphemous. I don't think that's the way it has to be—I think monotheism is compatible with tolerance and an appreciation of diversity—but the warning against conformism and repression of difference is well-taken.

---

94   GS 143
95   T III.1 and A 19

Nietzsche called Èzé a "marvelous Moorish eagle's nest."[96] The Moorish part is a little odd: The Moors did indeed occupy the place from the late 9th through most of the 10th century, but they didn't build it and nothing remains from their time here. All of the current buildings are late medieval, i.e. from at least two to four centuries later.

Still, Nietzsche definitely got the eagle's nest part right. This is the point at which the French Alps extend south far enough to reach the sea,[97] and at least as far back as Roman times this spot has been an invaluable lookout. From this high promontory at the edge of the mountains, hanging high above the coast, one would be able to see an enemy navy while it was still far out at sea, so far away that there would be time to run down the hill and alert the defenders on the coast. And the steep slopes surrounding the top of the mountain are so precipitous that the spot is easily defendable (although the natural defenses were not enough to keep the place from being conquered and re-conquered several times over the centuries, the last time by our friends the Savoys in the early 1700's).

We enter the oldest part of the town, the walled medieval city, through a 14th century postern gate and follow Avenue de Jardin Exotique as it winds around the hill, climbing gradually higher. *Vieux* Nice felt like an organic, interconnected structure, but this place all the more. In addition to the streets being non-linear and the buildings all built together and leaning on each other, we have the added element of verticality. Some alleys run up from the main street, others down. Some wind around and reconnect with other streets,

---

96   EH books.Z.4, as translated by Krell and Bates 222; Kaufman has "marvelous Moorish eyrie".

97   It's a pleasant coincidence—although part of the teaching of the eternal recurrence is that there's no such thing as coincidences—that the phrase "where the mountains meet the sea" is the slogan of Acadia National Park back home in Maine.

others lead only to unannounced dead-ends. Here and there we find stone barrels stuffed with bright red begonias, while sprays of pink bougainvillea spill over the tops of walls. Every so often between the buildings, there are glimpses of the surrounding hills or, if you're facing the right direction, the brilliant blue sea.

I have the feeling that I could explore here forever. Vicky, on the other hand, feels she could shop here forever. Just as the streets open up into unexpected little *places* and vantage-points, the shop-entrances reveal little havens of beautiful jewelry and clothing. Several contain artists' galleries.

We pass the Chapelle des Pénitents Blanc, home base of a 14th century monastic order whose main duty was tending to victims of the Black Plague (which is maybe why they called themselves the *white* penitents). This church was the site of the vote in which the residents of Èzé chose in 1860 unanimously to join Nice in taking on French rule. A little later we come to the 18th century church, Notre-Dame de l'Assomption, whose clock tower is Èzé le Village's tallest structure.

The avenue dead-ends at a turnstile and we pay a fee to enter the *jardin exotique*. What makes this garden exotic are the desert plants. These are not native to the Riviera, but on this exposed hilltop the sun is hot enough and the rain runs off quickly enough to allow desert plants to grow. Interspersed among the cacti are metal panels detailing the history of Èzé and some of the famous people who have visited and/or lived here; I am gratified to see that Nietzsche's visit is mentioned on three of the panels.

There is also a series of seven statues of female figures in honor of the goddess Isis, each with a metal panel inscribed with the statue's title and a little explanatory poem in both French and English. One of them, entitled "Justine as Isis," has this for its poem:

Vous m'avez reconnue …	You have recognized me …
Je suis la meme	I am the same
Et pourtant autre	And yet different

The meaning seems to be that the woman depicted in the sculpture resembles the goddess Isis and is perhaps her modern incarnation, so that we recognize the goddess in Justine. She is the same as the goddess and yet different, since she is Justine and not Isis. This is a nice illustration of Nietzsche's take on paganism, that it enables one to be an individual. Though this panel doesn't mention him, if anything it's an even nicer homage than the panels that do—evidence of someone following (probably unknowingly) in his footsteps.

Eventually we come to the top, the ruins of the 12th century castle. If the view we had from Gianton during our unintentional picnic was spectacular, the view from the very top of the hill is beyond spectacular. Down there the breadth of view was limited by hills on either side; up here one has a full 360 degrees. Almost half of the view is of the roofs of *le village*, the green hillside below, dotted with villas, and then the azure sea stretching to the infinite horizon. Behind us we see the rest of *le village* and the surrounding hills, including the Grande Corniche, the road from Nice to Monaco, built right into the hillside and held up by hidden arches and other architectural sleight-of-hand. The slope of the hill which we have ascended is so steep that where we now stand our feet are above the clock tower of the Church de l'Assomption, which just moments ago towered above us. We see how the deep blue of the clock's face matches the deep blue of the sea beyond. It is an amazing view, well worth the trip and the hike up, worth even eternal affirmation.

What do 21ˢᵗ century humans do at moments of affirmation? Take a picture, of course. We look around for someone to affirm for all eternity the presence of the Six Cohens atop Èzé. A fellow sees us looking around at people in this hopeful, inquiring, wordless way—it's really an unmistakable bit of universal body language, isn't it?—and says, "Would you like me to take your picture?"

"Um, sure," says Sam, as he hands over his camera. He bites his lip a little as he does so. His camera is brand-new, a thousand-dollar model in which he's invested several birthdays and Hanukkahs, in preparation for a stint at the Maine Media Workshop he'll attend later in the summer.

"You've picked the right person," says another man, "he's a professional—we're here for a family portrait." Sure enough, after snapping our picture and handing Sam's camera back, the photographer takes out his own and it's a mammoth, tricked-out model that Sam tells us later must have cost five thousand dollars or more. As the photographer turns to take the other family's photo with it, Sam's camera envy is hard to hide. "Nice camera, Sam," says Rosie.

And then down again, in search of a snack. We find a *crêperie* and take over three of the tiny outdoor tables squeezed along the sides of the street. Afterwards, fortified with crêpes in our bellies, we are ready for the *Sentier* Friedrich Nietzsche.

The descent begins at the edge of *le village*, just outside the postern gate of the medieval city. After just a few steps along the path we get a peek down into the terraced yard of a villa at the edge of the walled town. The lawn is a perfectly green patch of velvet. A mammoth chess set sits on a stone board at one side. It looks as if the pieces are three feet high.

Soon *le village* is left behind. A few more houses can be accessed from the path (and possibly also from roads or other paths out of sight), but soon we are on our own. Part of the path is wide and smooth with steps to help you along; part is narrow with loose gravel and rocks. All of it, however, is irresistibly scenic. We wind through a path between the hills, always with the fabulous sea before us, blue and beckoning— this is a major advantage to hiking down rather than up.

Yes, we are descending, not ascending, as Nietzsche did on this path, because we were worried that hiking up in the heat would spoil our enjoyment of the walled village. But now, as we stroll happily *down* the path, I find myself wondering if perhaps we weren't too cautious. We are technically in Nietzsche's footsteps, I suppose, since he most likely hiked down too, to return to the train station, rather than ride in the carriage. But we're not doing the half of the hike that matters most to the story, the upwards half. And the reason we're not doing it is that we played it safe and that seems unfaithful to the "live dangerously" aspect of Nietzsche's philosophy we discussed earlier. It seems like a betrayal, a sign of coal-like softness in the precise geographic location where Nietzsche urged diamond-like hardness. And so, in a deeper sense we're not really walking in Nietzsche's footsteps, even though we are on the same path.

This is one of those moments—if I may digress a little— which I've found to be endemic to philosophy, when your entire argument seems to fall to toothpicks. I can't count the number of times this has happened to me—writing papers for undergraduate courses, writing my senior thesis, writing papers for graduate courses, writing my dissertation, writing scholarly papers, writing my first book and now writing this book—but it seems to always happen that at some point I think again about what I'm saying and it seems to be pointless, trivial or just plain wrong. I bet this has happened to most working philosophers, maybe all, and maybe it happens to all of them all the time. There's something about philosophy that's precarious and risky—you're walking a thin tightrope without a net towards an endpoint you can't see. There's a sense in which philosophizing, though it's the paradigmatic armchair pursuit, is in fact a species of living dangerously.

Did Nietzsche feel these moments of self-doubt? I'll bet he did. His published writings all have an air of triumph, but that's because they're published—they're the successes. The existence of all his unpublished notebooks, including unused notes from all periods, unfinished outlines, unfinished projects, shows him flailing a good bit. Don't be fooled by the sheen of finished writing—the experience of one's argument falling to toothpicks is, I would guess, universal.

In my case, right now I've lost the path I had been walking. I had been saying that we were following in Nietzsche's footsteps because we were walking the very same path he walked. But I came a-cropper against the undeniable fact that we are walking it in a different direction than he did, at a different time of year and with a different purpose. And of course, he walked it alone while we are trekking as a family.

However, I would like to argue (having taken a moment to think and re-gather my toothpicks) that to walk the *chemin* Friedrich Nietzsche in our own way, taking into account our own particular circumstances, is *precisely* to walk in his footsteps, since he walked it in *his* own way, taking into account *his* own particular circumstances. He walked that path in winter with no children and at a different age than all of us (older than the children, younger than Vicky and me), and in a state of mind where he saw his culture going slack and wanted to resist that decline by deliberately seeking out challenges. In his situation, climbing was appropriate. Our situation, coming to Èzé in the summer with children, at a different age and with a different agenda, is different from his and so it's fitting to respond differently. On reflection, I do think it's appropriate for us to play it a little safe, given our weaknesses of age and heat-resistance and our desire not to spoil our day, one of our precious few on this special trip, by pushing ourselves too hard.

I thus come to the view that, in the deepest sense, our walking down instead of up actually puts us right in Nietzsche's footsteps, metaphorically speaking. He was doing his own thing, not following the crowd, and we are doing our own thing, not following the crowd (which in this case is Nietzsche). And I think that's his ultimate message, the point of the passage he wrote while on that hillside. Hardness is not just physical, not just a matter of hiking up instead of down; it's also mental, a matter of doing the individual thing, the thing appropriate just for you, rather than following someone else. In that sense we *did* think for ourselves. And it's the thinking for oneself that matters, not the particular content of what one does.

Perhaps this is the counterbalance to what was said earlier about communing with Nietzsche by visiting the places he lived and walking the paths he walked. Such following threatens to disqualify our individualism. And so, we re-assert our individualism by visiting Nietzsche's haunts in our own way—doing the same thing, but differently. And hopefully we do it in a way that is still a challenge in some sense, still something that will promote our idiosyncratic growth (although as we walk down this not-especially-difficult path I must admit I'm a little bit uncertain about that).

Strictly speaking, of course, you *can't* imitate another's example, try as you might. We could have taken the train, hiked up, even written something in our pocket notebooks as we climbed and still not be imitating Nietzsche because of our different ages, the different time of year, and so forth. There are always differences between any two people's experiences, even between the two experiences the same person might have while trying to recreate his/her own prior experience (for example, if Nietzsche had walked the path a second time, say, which for all I know he may have actually done). This doesn't stop people from trying of course, and Nietzsche's excoriation of conformists as "herd animals" is, if anything from this standpoint, even more deserved. You literally *can't* imitate someone else's example, so the attempt to do so is not only craven, stemming from fear of standing out and being your own person, but irrational, since it's impossible.

This is the true paradox of individualism: The only way to be a unique individual is to be unlike anyone else, as any unique individual would. It's kind of like that statue up in the Jardin Exotique, "Justine as Isis: I am the same and yet different." But Nietzsche himself puts it best (of course!) in a very short passage entitled "Imitators," featuring a mock dialogue between A and B:

> A: What? You want no imitators?
> B: I do not want to have people imitate
> my example; I wish that everybody should
> fashion his own example, as *I* do.
> A: So?[98]

Once we accept the paradox as inevitable, it becomes clear that it's the manner of fashioning that's crucial, not the content of the action. Then, if the content of the action happens to match someone else's (or not)—well, that's not the crucial thing. The crucial thing is thinking for oneself.

One final thought about this issue of hiking down instead of up: At the very beginning of *Thus Spoke Zarathustra*, the title character comes down from his mountain to bring his message to all. In parallel fashion, we walked down the *chemin* Friedrich Nietzsche, not up, and I'm bringing you

---

98   GS 255

Nietzsche's message. I could be spending my time writing my own aphorisms, remaining atop the intellectual mountain. Instead I have chosen to come down from that mountain and devote myself in this book to sharing some of Nietzsche's philosophy with non-specialists.

Robert Pirsig, in *Zen and the Art of Motorcycle Maintenance*—the book which, in the summer between freshman and sophomore year, turned me into a philosophy major—likens philosophy to a mountain peak. Though barren itself, in the sense that it never successfully answers its own questions (which is why we're still, thousands of years after Socrates, wondering what truth is, or what the best life is), philosophy defines the shape of the rest of the mountain, i.e. the surrounding culture. In this way, philosophy spins off the specialized sciences—physics, economics, psychology, *et al*, which were all done originally by philosophers—and contributes ideas to the rest of culture while itself remaining barren.

It's always seemed to me, following this metaphor, that different people are comfortable on different parts of the mountain. Some, i.e. the most abstract philosophers, like the very top, above the tree line, where the view is biggest but there's also nothing growing. Other philosophers like to move down a little ways—still with a view, but returning to earth, looking outwards and downwards. Other people, in other fields of inquiry, of science, of creativity, etc., like the sides of the mountain or its foothills, or even the valleys defined by the mountain and watered by its run-off, where fertility is greatest.

I like heading downwards. Climbing hurts my knees. But I do like being up high with big views. I'm not a philosophical innovator, but I offer Nietzsche's philosophy to you here as a trail you might want to walk yourself sometime too, in your own way which fits the circumstances of your own life, of course. Thus, in following Nietzsche's footsteps, I make my *own* meaning in life, quite different from his. And in this way, I follow his example.

NOW then, back to the path. All this re-enactment of the paradox of individualism has brought us to about halfway down the hill. Time for a drink and a rest and a minute to commune with Nietzsche. We find large rocks or clear spaces on the ground on which to sit and everyone pulls out a water bottle and a snack. I pull out the passage from *Ecce Homo*, cited in *The Good European*, about Nietzsche's climb to Èzé and read it to the kids:

> The following winter [i.e. 1883-4], under the halcyon skies of Nice, which glistened above me for the first time in my life, I discovered the third part of *Zarathustra*— and the book was finished. Scarcely a year for the composition of the whole. Many concealed spots and many heights in the landscape of Nice have become sacrosanct to me because of the unforgettable moments there. That decisive part of the third book, "Of Old and New Tablets," was composed on the difficult and steep ascent from the railway station at Èzé to the marvelous Moorish eagle's nest overhead. My muscle tone was always greatest when my creative energies flowed most abundantly. *The body* is spirited—let us leave the 'soul' out of play.... One could often have spotted me dancing:

> at that time I could wander through the
> mountains for seven or eight hours at a time
> without tiring. I slept well, I laughed a lot—I
> was as fit as I could be, and I was patient.[99]

The children listen carefully and have questions similar to those I've talked about above.

"What's in 'Of Old and New Tablets?'" asks Sam.

Well, there's a lot in it, I reply—it's the longest section in the entire book and touches on many of the themes of Nietzsche's philosophy—but it's the last part that's most relevant. And then I read them the "Why so hard? Why so soft?" passage I quoted above.

"Kind of like letting someone else do something for you instead of doing it yourself," says Eli.

"Or reading a summary of a book instead of the book itself," says Rosie. "Why does he call it 'Moorish?'" she adds. I don't have a good explanation for that. Nietzsche may just have been responding to how exotic the place felt to him.

"How come he claims to be healthy?" wonders Vicky. "Didn't you say he was on a disability pension?"

"He was sick a lot," I say, "but when he was healthy he was a terrific walker," and I promise more proof of this when we get to the Alps.

We resume after the break. The path ceases switch-backing and heads westward towards *la gare*. At the very bottom the path is paved and runs through a small residential section. The descent takes us about an hour. Going up would probably have been an hour and a half or more and the midday heat might well have sapped our spirits for enjoying Èzé. In the end we feel we planned well. If I were to do it again—and I hope I will!—I would leave early in the day so as to be able

---

99   EH books.Z.4, as translated by Krell & Bates 222

to walk up in the cool of morning, then have a much more leisurely time up top before descending again at evening.

We catch the bus back to town and find a supper of exotic Niçoise specialties: chickpea-flour crêpes called *socca*, caramelized onion flatbread called *pissaladiere*, and a deep-fried yeast dough pastry called *beignets*. They make a fitting end to our fabulous day trip to Èzé. We lost time because of my bus mistake, but we still got to visit a beautiful old town with jaw-dropping hilltop views of the sea and to take a literal walk in Nietzsche's footsteps. I'd be happy to do it all again, both soon and eternally.

Nice *Moderne:*
Nietzsche & the Artist

AFTER A LONG day yesterday and a lot of Nietzsche, today will be quieter and more focused on the family. Of course, you never know when he might pop up unexpectedly.

Our breakfast conversation concerns our plans for the day. Just as the Èzé pilgrimage was my primary goal in Nice, for Vicky and Rosie it is going to the craft booths which take over the Cours Saleya on Thursday evenings. So that part of the day gets set first. And for the morning? Sam, our photography buff, wants to see the *Théâtre de la photographie et l'image*. I'm hankering for an art museum, and Eli and Miriam like the idea of a park. So I open up the various maps we've collected and see what can be worked out. I find that Sam's gallery is just a few blocks north of us and that if we keep walking in that same direction, we will come eventually to the Musée Chagall. Then there's a bus that goes even further in that same direction and eventually goes past the Parc des Arènes de Cimiez.

Walking north means we're pointed away from the old city and heading into Nice *moderne*, which in this part of the world means 19th century. The building housing the *Théâtre de la photographie et l'image* on boulevard Dubouchage was originally a Belle Epoque villa—probably brand-new in Nietzsche's day—converted into a theater in 1911 and now used for projecting art films and hosting a small photographic gallery.

At the gallery is a wall-sized print of several fashion models striding towards the camera. To the right of it is the exact same photo of the models in exactly the same positions, but in the nude.

"Sorry," whispers Sam, "I didn't know that photo would be here." He's thinking of twelve-year-old Eli and ten-year-old Miriam but really, we all take it in stride (so to speak). It's just the human body, we tell him—no reason to be embarrassed. Openness works best in these sorts of situations. If one reacts with embarrassment, it gets transmitted. Meanwhile, the photos present an interesting juxtaposition in which one realizes that under the fashionable clothes are real human animals and that one has been paying attention to them without actually seeing them. This pair of photos, in fact, seem precisely situated within one of Nietzsche's self-proclaimed projects, mentioned earlier, to "translate man back into nature." The recognition prompted by the photos, he might say, is one we all should have. The camera is able to see the women as they are, without societal expectation. That stance of open, unprejudiced seeing is one we would do well to adopt.

We exit the building—Sam still sheepish—and walk further north through a more commercial area and eventually climb a stone staircase from a side street up to the Boulevard de Cimiez. Two days ago, descending a staircase to enter the *vielle ville,* we stepped backwards in time. Now, ascending a staircase, we step forwards from the 19th century into the 20th. The surroundings are green and elegant—Cimiez is one of Nice's classiest neighborhoods. We finish our walk at the Musée Chagall.

The painter Marc Chagall was Jewish, born in Russia, but spent most of his life in France and his most creative years in Provence, so Nice is a most appropriate place for a museum devoted to his work.

Most of Chagall's paintings recall the artist's home territory of shtetls and poor farmers, but the paintings also feature flying donkeys, cows and other farm animals; impossibly constructed streets and barns; and floating people, often couples, draped in strands of vines and flowers. The paintings are often difficult to decipher, but even if all one comprehends is a portion here and a portion there, what's depicted is charming and the colors are among the most brilliant an artist has ever used. Rosie, who has a mild degree of synesthesia, is particularly fascinated by the colors. She seems drawn into them, something like the character in Mark Helprin's *A Winter's Tale* who has "color gravity." She'll walk up close to them and just stare. Eli and Miriam have some trouble appreciating what's going on, but Vicky talks them through what they see—over here is a recognizable scene, over there are some friendly looking farm animals. Here and there are paintings with Biblical references and we focus on these as familiar ground.

Many artists, especially the German expressionists, have been inspired by Nietzsche's work, though he himself had relatively little to say about painting. His poor eyesight is surely most of the story. In a letter to his mother from Nice, he describes the rug in his new lodgings as simply "of a dark color."[100] To be sure, in another letter he writes, "[T]here can be no more beautiful season in Nice than the current one: the sky blindingly white, the sea tropical blue, and in the night a moonlight that makes the gas lanterns feel ashamed, for they flush red."[101] So he might well have loved Chagall's bright colors. But I also suspect he would have found the artist's self-referential symbolism indulgent.

100   Letter of December 10, 1885, in Krell & Bates 192
101   Letter to Malwida von Meysenbug December 13, 1886, in Krell & Bates 221

By what right do I make such a statement? I can't point to a passage where Nietzsche says he finds self-referential symbolism in paintings self-indulgent. There are some places where he criticizes self-indulgence in artists—most of them aimed at Wagner. But I think ultimately what I'm relying on even more is something I call my "inner Nietzschean voice".

I noticed myself growing such a voice during my senior year in college. In the fall, I took a course entirely devoted to Nietzsche and then in the spring wrote my senior thesis on him. So in a period of about four months I read most of what he had written that was available at that time in English via the Kaufmann translations. It seemed to me then that I could tell what Nietzsche would say about something, not by finding a particular passage that referred to it, but just by reaching into that part of me that had absorbed his viewpoint. It seemed like there was a Nietzsche center set up in a part of my brain and I could consult it from the inside.

What words does this voice tell me? I imagine a lot of people think it nasty and derisive—that's a popular image of Nietzsche, the man who declared the death of God and wrote a book entitled *The Antichrist*, etc. Early in my senior year of college, when I was just starting to get to know Nietzsche and work up some understanding of him for my senior thesis, I went to a family gathering where a relative said, "Oh, you're studying Nietzsche? You should talk to cousin So-and-so— he's into Nietzsche." So I found this cousin and told him I was learning about Nietzsche and was trying to figure out all the different interpretations. I asked him if he had any advice for me. He told me, "My advice is—get your own interpretation and fuck everybody."

There's something of the Nietzschean spirit in that remark, to be sure. But Nietzsche himself was not like that at all—he would never use such language, for example. Accounts by people who knew him report him to be polite and gracious, especially to women, despite some of the aggressively chauvinistic things he said about them in print. So it's got to be more complex than that. When you read a lot of his work, it becomes clear that while he does have a penchant for and enjoyment of overturning ideologies and institutions, it comes as a result of long and sensitive thinking about them, and often with a good bit of respect for the purposes they served in their time. For example, even though religion is one of his favorite targets, he recognizes its role in creating European culture:

> The long unfreedom of the spirit, the mistrustful constraint in the communicability of thoughts, the discipline thinkers imposed on themselves to think within the directions laid down by a church or court... the long spiritual will to interpret all events under a Christian schema and to rediscover and justify the Christian god in every accident— all this, however forced, capricious, hard, gruesome, and anti-rational, has shown itself to be the means through which the European spirit has been trained to strength, ruthless curiosity, and subtle mobility.... That for thousands of years European thinkers thought merely in order to prove something ... that the conclusions that *ought* to be the result of their most rigorous reflection were always settled from the start ...—this tyranny, this caprice, this rigorous and grandiose stupidity has *educated* the spirit.[102]

So I would say the Nietzschean spirit is less a matter of reckless overturning and more a matter of looking at things in a clear-eyed and non-romanticized way in order to evaluate them without prejudice. Nietzsche describes it himself in *Beyond Good and Evil* via a passage from Stendahl, which he quotes in the original French (thus making it especially appropriate for me to quote while we're here in Nice):

> *Pour être un bon philosophe, il faut être sec, clair, sans illusion. Un banquier, qui a fait fortune, a une partie du caractère requis pour faire des découvertes en philosophie, c'est-à-dire pour voir clair dans ce qui est.*

[And then here is Kaufmann's translation of the passage]

> To be a good philosopher, one must be dry, clear, without illusion. A banker who has made a fortune has one character trait that is needed for making discoveries in philosophy, that is to say, for seeing clearly into what is.[103]

That's the key to the Nietzschean voice, I think—not necessarily discarding everything established, but having the freedom and clear-eyed view of things that would make discarding possible; or if one decides to affirm them instead, to do so with full knowledge and justification, not just out of habit or weakness or conformism or fear of novelty.

---

103   BGE 39

FROM Musée Chagall we take the bus on a straight shot up the boulevard to the top of the hill. Cimiez is now just a neighborhood of Nice, but in Roman times it was a separate settlement called Cemenelum. What remains of the Roman period is an amphitheater and some other ruins. The amphitheater is the anchor of a park where we find lunch, including another Niçoise specialty, *tarte aux blettes*, as well as the kids' third tomato/basil/mozzarella panini in three days.

Right next door is the Musée Matisse, in an old 19th Century mansion. This is another of the art museums I'm hankering for. I want to drop in, but the group overrules me—they want "feet-up" time before we head out again for the evening, so they ask me to consult my maps to find a bus to take us back to our apartment. The will of the group trumps the will of the individual and so I am deflected from my art lover self back to my usual role as family navigator.

Is this an annoying block to what I would do if I were on my own, or is it an opportunity to affirm the importance of other people in my life? Is family a hindrance to a writer's life, or a support? Am I being unfaithful to Nietzsche by subordinating my individual side to the group, or am I being faithful to him by pursuing my own path in life, one that—contrary to his own example, but still something I definitely affirm—involves sticking by people with whom one has established a relationship, a mutual reliance? In this highly individualistic age—more people living alone than ever before, finding their meaning in life solo, etc. (one of the clearest respects in which the world walks in Nietzsche's footsteps, incidentally)—perhaps one can go one's own way precisely by rejecting individualism and devoting oneself to one's relationships. Or maybe not. This tension in my life, continually renewed, continually perplexes me. Nietzsche is clear that we are the artists of our own lives, but after a morning in the art world, my personal painting seems to me as puzzling as a flying donkey.

To put the matter another way: Nietzsche says, "Be yourself." But who the hell is that? Which me am I supposed to be right now? My hero gives no answers.

THE bus takes a switchback route down the hill on Avenue des Arènes de Cimiez, emerging finally near the Musée d'Art Moderne et Contemporain, a strikingly new building, and another reminder that this is not merely an ossified tourist town.

Of course, I have to say I *like* ossified tourist towns, so I am glad when feet-up time is over to be walking back through the *vielle ville*. We've decided to follow feet-up time with feet-wet time—that is, we've decided to sample the beach. We didn't pack swimsuits, since we knew we would have at most just a few minutes out of our two weeks to use them, but nevertheless we want to at least dip our toes in the Mediterranean. The beach is crowded and stony. Barefoot, we pick our way gingerly across the rocks and delicately around the towels bearing near-naked people. The water is surprisingly chilly—thinking this was *southern* France, I had expected bath water—but of course not nearly as chilly as the ocean in Maine.

We had heard that women often went topless at this beach—and if you think viewing art photographs of naked supermodels with your ten-year-old daughter is awkward, try going to a topless beach with your wife—but we find little evidence of this practice. I wonder what Nietzsche would think of the idea of a topless beach. I suppose he might have approved of it philosophically, in principle. After all, what's more natural than nakedness? On the other hand, one of the things that has developed naturally through the course of human history is the institution of clothing and a general convention about which parts of the body can or cannot be displayed publicly (differing by culture and time period of course, but still, there's always some convention or other). What I'm pretty sure of, though, is that the actual Nietzsche himself, man of the 19th century that he was, would have been scandalized. Victorianism pervaded Europe far beyond England, and Nietzsche himself had as bourgeois an upbringing as anyone else of that time. He struggled to free himself of bourgeois repression to be sure, and he wrote often of the importance of having a more natural attitude towards the body and all things physical. But if he had ever seen in reality something like the bodily display common on Riviera beaches today, he would surely have been unable to handle it. Not that we 21st century post-Victorians should feel superior. Enlightened though we think we are, it's not clear we handle the idea of the naked body that much better, or even if we do, it's not clear we are all that much better off.

WE are too early for the arts and craft vendors, so we climb the Colline de Chateau, the hill where the Savoy castle used to stand before the French destroyed it in 1706, now a park. Somewhere up here is a place named Terrasse Friedrich Nietzsche, but I don't spend any time looking for it. I had been discouraged by the maps, which are unclear as to where it is exactly. At any rate, this Terrasse doesn't mark any particular place in Nietzsche's personal history, as the *Sentier* does; it's just an effort by the municipality to note his famous presence in the city, and the fact that he took walks up here (the *colline*

is situated between his residence on Rue Catherine Segurane and the *vielle ville*). The view west is breathtaking, however, and we take some photos of the sunset.

Back down in the Cours Saleya, the females of the family cruise the arts and crafts vendors while the boys and I find a place out of the bustle to people-watch. In retrospect, this is another moment I should have felt my Nietzschean self being constrained by family. On my own I would have moved on, perhaps to stroll the *Promenade des Anglais* in the direction of the setting sun. After all, those are genuine footsteps of Friedrich too, just as much as the *Sentier* in Èzé.

But I was fine with it just then. As I think about it, as a solitary person Nietzsche was in the position of people-watcher often—in the hotel dining room, sitting in a café, strolling the streets—so this too is an activity which is in his footsteps, metaphorically speaking. I find it easy to imagine sitting with him in such moments, at a *café*, on any *parc* bench; we'd share people-watching observations, and other thoughts as well. He'd be full of ideas and provocative conversation, ready to share his most recent notebook passage, his eyes twinkling over that outrageous mustache. And though I wouldn't be able to keep up on his walks—he was tall and long-legged and vigorous, when healthy—I'd take my own walks, strolling the boulevards, *plassas*, and pedestrian walkways, poking around the winding warren of the *vielle ville*, stretching out my stride along the Promenade des Anglais, hiking up the Colline du Chateau, and then have my own thoughts and record them in my own journal.

I did in fact live that way, for a short time, doing nothing but walking and thinking and writing in my notebook—thoughts that crystallized in a satisfying way, observations about the world, insights into myself. I did this most intensively in Europe after graduating college: I roamed through Paris, Clery-du-Bords, Clermont-Ferrand, the Parc de Volcans, Perigeux, then across the channel to London, Brighton, and Cambridge. Most of that time was spent just looking for a good place to sit and write in my notebook. That's all that mattered back then. What amazes me about that mode of life now, above all, is how I would consider it a good day simply by dint of having had a good thought. That's all it took to make life valuable, to make a day good— having a good thought. What a wonderful way to live! I could still live that way, alone with my notebook, the way Nietzsche did; I'm sure I could.

But my mode of life no longer revolves around this activity, because I chose to enter the world. I chose to have a family, a career, and engage in all sorts of other social relations, and by remaining engaged with these relations, I am continually re-choosing them. Nietzsche left those things behind, partly out of choice and partly out of necessity, and that's when his note-booking began. I, on the other hand, left note-booking behind to have those things. Which of us was/is better off? Nietzsche collapsed after fourteen years of living that way, whereas here I am still alive. On the other hand, I sometimes feel out of touch with an essential part of me, estranged from a mode of life that's incredibly precious.

Ascent: Nice to Turin

NIETZSCHE'S TRANSFER from Nice to Turin in April 1888 was marred by his getting on the wrong train when changing in Genoa. Ours, in June 2008, is marred by a forty-minute delay in Nice because the train doors aren't operational. After weeks of my telling the kids to prepare themselves for the power and glory of European trains, *this* happens. The air conditioning doesn't work either, so we swelter as we sit in the station. This is the same station whose expansion resulted in the demolition of Nietzsche's residence on the petite Rue St. Etienne. The thought occurs to me that perhaps its ruins are underneath the very spot on which our train sits motionless. Eventually we are directed to switch to a different train on a different platform—on which the doors work but again not the air conditioning—and eventually we set off slowly, carrying the heat with us.

The trip is disappointing. The train's route runs right along the coast of the Riviera and I had been anticipating a series of spectacular views. It turns out that most of our views are of the insides of tunnels carved from the hills that go right down to the water's edge. The tunnels reek, yet we have to keep the windows open in order to keep the air circulating. We don't get so much as a glance at Monaco even when the train stops there, because the train station is underground, and the story is the same on the Italian side at San Remo.

There are enough above-ground stretches for us to see that

the French Riviera looks a lot wealthier than the Italian. Even though these two territories were ruled together for much of the past millennium by the House of Savoy, by now the different fortunes and economies of France and Italy have had their effect, and there is a clearly visible change as we cross the current border. Buildings on the French side are generally better maintained and there's more decorative greenery as well. The Italian buildings are more likely to be run-down, crumbling and surrounded by dusty empty lots. However, on the Italian side people seem to be actually utilizing their balconies to a much greater extent. Most of them have flower pots, chairs and drying laundry. The Italian balconies look like places where life is actually lived, not just real estate holdings. Noting the rundown condition of the buildings, I share with my current family a memory from the time my birth family traveled to Italy when I was in my twenties.

"We would often go to some tourist site and find that it was closed for restorations. It seemed like everywhere we went, there'd be a sign saying *chiuso per restauro*. It was like some kind of joke. Over and over, when we would enter an old church, or turn the corner in an art museum looking for a certain gallery, or whatever, we would find a sign saying *chiuso per restauro*. Seeing all these rundown buildings makes me think we should be prepared for the same thing in Turin." My current family nods and returns to their train activities.

And it occurs to me, having just recounted an experience I had in Italy with my birth family to my current family, who are just now entering Italy for the first time, and reflecting on my passage from the one to the other, that Nietzsche had the former but not the latter, and thus missed out on something that has been a huge aspect of my life. For that matter, he doesn't write a lot about birth families, and this is kind of surprising since he is very curious about the origins of

things—morals most famously, but many other things too—
and birth families are surely huge in everyone's story. There
is, to be sure, a fascinating aphorism in an early work about
children living out tensions between their parents:

> *Continuance of the parents*—The
> unresolved dissonances between the
> characters and dispositions of the parents
> continue to resound in the nature of the
> child and constitute the history of his inner
> sufferings.[104]

This is insightful, I think. I see it in my own oscillations
between my father's self-confidence and my mother's stoicism,
and in Vicky's alternations between her mother's thrift and
her father's prodigality. But when, ten years after writing the
preceding aphorism, Nietzsche finally gets around to writing
his autobiography, he claims that the dissonance between his
parents was one of his greatest pieces of luck:

> The good fortune of my existence, its
> uniqueness perhaps, lies in its fatality: I am,
> to express it in the form of a riddle, already
> dead as my father, while as my mother I
> am still living and becoming old. This dual
> descent, as it were, both from the highest
> and the lowest rung on the ladder of life, at
> the same time a *decadent* and a *beginning*—
> this, if anything, explains that neutrality,
> that freedom from all partiality in relation
> to the total problem of life, that perhaps
> distinguishes me. I have a subtler sense of
> smell for the signs of ascent and decline than

any other human being before me; I am the
teacher *par excellence* for this—I know both,
I am both.[105]

So is he saying parental tensions are a good thing or a
bad thing? And if the point is not to label tensions as wholly
good or wholly bad but rather to affirm the dissonances by
turning them into fully harmonized counterpoints, could
Nietzsche please say a little more about how his own struggle
worked itself out and/or give us another example? He does
not. Of all his other relatives he mentions only one other, a
grandmother—his father's mother, through whom he claims
to be connected to various notables, including Goethe. He
never mentions his sister, his dead brother or the maiden
aunts who shared the house during his childhood, or the
interpersonal dynamics between any of these people. Bookish
intellectual that he was, he may well have been oblivious to
these things. Still, sensitive as he clearly is to the influence of
his own parentage on his life, it's a shame that he never offers
any deeper or more general discussion of this universal life
experience.

Approaching Genoa, we roll past a spot where two sets
of tracks merge together in front of a small brick building
labeled Sampierdarena. I recognize the name. This was where
Nietzsche wound up a hundred and twenty years ago, after
getting confused in Genoa and boarding the wrong train on
his way from Nice to Turin. At the time Sampierdarena was
a separate town. Now, given Genoa's urban sprawl, it's just
a rail junction on the outskirts of the city. When Nietzsche
got off the train he had mistakenly boarded, he took out his
frustration by ranting at the innocent natives of the town.
This, in turn, brought on a two-day migraine. So Nietzsche

---

105   EH wise.1

wound up spending two nights at an inn in Sampierdarena with the very same people he had just reamed out.

In our case, the damage caused by our travel snafu is that we miss the train we had expected to catch and so lose the reserved seats we had expected to sit in. Instead of making a quick connection to an express train, sitting in comfortable seats and arriving in Turin with plenty of time to get settled and still make something of the day, we stand on a crowded platform in Genoa for twenty minutes, then ride to Turin on a local train, making many more stops and moving much slower than the earlier train would have. In the end we don't reach Turin until late afternoon.

Weary and sweaty, the Professional Travelers extend the handles on our rollaboards, rumble down the platform, navigate our way through Stazione di Porta Nuova—much of which, sure enough, is covered in scaffolding—and emerge onto the streets of Turin.

NIETZSCHE'S love for Turin began with the conditions for walking, both below his feet and above his head. Below his feet were wide, smooth paving stones. His eyes by this time were so bad that he was prone to trip on obstacles as he walked, so these trustworthy pavers were quite welcome. Meanwhile, above his head were the famous covered porticos of Turin, eighteen kilometers' worth, providing ceilings for the sidewalks along all of the main streets in the center of town and even, in many cases, covering the street crossings as well. This meant he could undertake his daily walks regardless of the weather, and even go quite far.

The porticos begin right across Corso Vittorio Emmanuel from the Porto Nuova train station (that is, that's the place they begin from our *perspective*, entering Turin from that direction). They are both wide and high. I've always felt that I stand taller when provided with a high ceiling, and these elegant arches make me feel ennobled as I walk under them. The pillars supporting the arches are thick and strong, the spaces between them often filled with display cases or seating for shops or cafes on the opposite side of the arcade. Although Chicago is known as the city of broad shoulders, I actually feel the epithet applies better to Turin.

On our initial stroll, pulling our rollaboards, we walk only as far as Via Cavour. Count Camillo Cavour was the statesman who guided the drive for Italian independence in the 1850's and 60's. Among other things, he negotiated the deal that transferred Nice to the French to ensure French support for Vittorio Emmanuel's claims to rule Italy. So our arrival route—ending our rail journey from Nice by crossing Corso Vittorio Emmanuel to get to Via Cavour—is a happy historical coincidence. Cavour's own house is on this very street, just a few meters from our apartment. A couple days from now we will poke our heads into the courtyard and gaze at the elegant staircases going up and out of sight to both left and right.

But right now, we're hot and we're tired and we want to get to our apartment already.

We find the door to our building—a small cutout inside a large, garage-sized door, with a big brass knob right in the middle—and enter. In the entranceway to the left is the superintendent's office, and our adventures in Italian begin. So this is the right time to talk about how we handled the language issue on our trip.

I said at the beginning of this book that part of the appeal of this particular itinerary was the fact that we would be in three different language zones: French, Italian, and German.

We decided when we started planning the trip that the six of us would split into pairs, with each pair responsible for handling that language. Sam and Rosie were studying French in school, so they formed that pair and they did fine. Meanwhile, Vicky, who had taken German at the Salzburg Institute years ago, said she'd be happy to refresh her knowledge, and Eli joined her in the German pair.

I elected to take on Italian. In my previous trips to Italy I had felt estranged from the world around me, unable to understand even advertising billboards. So I had promised myself that I wouldn't go back without learning some Italian, and so that became my responsibility, and Miriam joined me to make the Italian pair. We got a Berlitz CD from the public library and practiced in the car. It went OK—we learned how to count and make simple conversation. So when we enter the doorway to our apartment building I am feeling pretty confident.

But it all goes 'poof' when the superintendent, Maria, comes out of her office to greet us. For one thing, I'm completely bushed, drained by the heat and the overlong journey. But the much larger factor is that, despite dutiful work with Berlitz and the phrasebooks, it turns out I am utterly unprepared.

Italian looks easy on paper, since every letter is pronounced (unlike French), and the letters always take the same sounds (unlike English), and the words usually have English cognates, or if not resemble words in other Romance languages or in Latin (I had five years of Latin in high school). And the Berlitz CD featured people speaking slowly and repeating themselves, even for easy things like *"Buona sera, Matteo."* But *actual* Italians speaking *actual* Italian is a whole other thing. The Italians revel in the musicality of their language, emphasizing certain sounds and dropping the volume way down for others, with elegant little trills and accents thrown in throughout. It's beautiful to listen to, and Italians' sheer enjoyment of language and speech is wonderful. You come to understand, too, why Italian is the primary language of opera, since it's full of vowels that keep your mouth open and allow for embellishment. The way ordinary Italians in ordinary situations essentially *sing* their sentences makes for a very small leap to the opera house. But it also makes it hard for a newcomer to hear, or at least it was beyond *this* newcomer's ability at this late hour.

So when Maria, the superintendent, a lovely, dark-haired woman, steps out of her office, here's how my conversation with her goes:

Me: Buongiorno! (cautiously, trying to sound like Matteo on the CD)

Maria: BuonGIOR-no! (she, on the other hand, throws her whole self into the word)

Me: Famiglia Cohen? (gesturing to all of us)

Maria: Ah, faMI-glia CO-hen!

Me: Jonathan, Victoria, Sam, Rosa, Eli, e Miriam.

Maria: BIEN-venI-di! (At this point Maria says some other stuff which I can't quite catch, but at the end she says) CIN-que NOZ-ze?

Me: Si, cinque nozze. (I can repeat her last words—it's like following the CD.)

Maria: (But then she says some more stuff, and then some more stuff, and it all sounds, given the musical tone and dynamics of her delivery, like the recitative from an opera, maybe *La Traviata*, but at the end I hear something like) SeGUI-mi a gli apPAR-taMENT-i.

Maria then sings some other things and like a good opera performer accompanies her words with gestures, in this case towards the stairs and the elevator. Apparently, this all means we should follow her up to the apartments, which is what we do next.

Maria has by now sung a couple hundred words at least, and I have understood exactly ten of them. But nobody's gotten hurt and we have all managed to wind up upstairs together, so I suppose we're doing fine so far.

Our apartments are two small, but perfectly serviceable rooms next to each other at the end of a corridor. One has a sticker of a Jewish star on it, which gives us some pause. The sight reminds me that we are in the land that produced *The Garden of the Finzi-Continis*, a beautiful film which depicts an Italian Jewish family living an illusory life, safe behind their garden wall, on the eve of the Holocaust. Italian fascism was not intrinsically anti-Semitic the way German fascism was, but still, the Italians did get on board with it once they allied themselves with the Nazis. Has this door for some reason been labeled in advance of our arrival? Vicky is clearly thinking the same thing. She gives me a look, then points and asks Maria what this is. Maria replies, "*STEL-la*," which in the dictionary means "star". Right, I think—it's just a star. Silly to connect it with the Finzi-Continis—this is 65 years later, a whole new Europe.

It's similar, by the way, with Nietzsche and anti-Semitism. He's associated with it in the popular imagination because of his sister's misrepresentation, which allowed him to be used in Nazi propaganda; but the association falls away as soon as you read any of his work. If anything, he goes out of his way to invert stereotypes and embarrass the anti-Semites of his day. As an example, at the end of the first essay in *On the Genealogy of Morals*, after giving an account which traces a tension between values in our moral life back to the ancient world, Nietzsche writes the following:

Which of them has won *for the present*, Rome or Judea? But there can be no doubt: consider to whom one bows down in Rome itself today, as if they were the epitome of the highest values—and not only in Rome but over almost half the earth, everywhere that man has become tame or desires to become tame: *three Jews* ... and *one Jewess* (Jesus of Nazareth, the fisherman Peter, the rug weaver Paul, and the mother of the aforementioned Jesus, Mary). This is very remarkable: Rome has been defeated beyond all doubt.[106]

So the negative points he makes about the values he traces back to ancient Judea (and "become tame" is one of the mildest, believe me), which might give ammunition to contemporary anti-Semites, he now makes clear are directed not against Judaism but against Christianity. Or again, later in *Genealogy*:

I do not like the 'New Testament,' that should be plain; I find it almost disturbing that my taste in regard to this most highly esteemed and overestimated work should be so singular (I have the taste of two millennia *against* me): but there it is! 'Here I stand, I cannot do otherwise.'[107]—I have the courage of my bad taste. The *Old* Testament—that is something else again: all honor to the Old Testament! I find in it great human beings, a

---

106   GM I.16
107   Quoting Martin Luther in a screed against the New Testament is a typically cheeky Nietzschean move.

heroic landscape, and something of the very rarest quality in the world, the naïveté of the *strong heart*; what is more, I find a people. In the New one, on the other hand, I find nothing but petty sectarianism, mere rococo of the soul, mere involutions, queer things, the air of the conventicle, not to forget an occasional whiff of bucolic mawkishness that belongs to the epoch … and is not so much Jewish as Hellenistic.[108]

Make no mistake: Nietzsche has plenty of negative things to say about religion. In the *Genealogy* he traces the concepts of sin, ritual purity, the morality of humility, etc.—three things he thinks particularly hamper contemporary culture —to their ancient Jewish roots. But those criticisms are launched as a philosophical attack on all forms of monotheism. The latter may well have been initiated by Jews, but attacking it is not anti-Semitism.

WE ENTER the first apartment where Maria, strangely inspired by the plain furniture and dingy surroundings, decides it would be a good time to deliver another opera *recitativo*, which I don't recognize but think might possibly be from *La Tosca*. We move on to the second room, where she switches over to *Il barbiere di Siviglia.* I have no idea what she's saying, but the rooms appear to be okay, so I'm not too worried about it.

There is a washing machine in the second apartment, and I am thinking that in light of our continual need to do laundry it would be nice to know how to work it—*really* know, not just know it in translation—so I ask her in English, hoping against hope that this will somehow help *my* understanding. Maria seems to understand "washing machine" well enough to go stand in front of it and point to it, somewhat like an infomercial presenter trying to sell it to me. For some reason this encourages me. It turns out however, that the instructions to the washing machine are simply a sampling of arias from *Il Trovatore*. As opera, it's probably terrific. As instructions for using a washing machine, it's pretty much incomprehensible. When Maria finishes I nod and thank her, although I really feel like applauding and throwing roses onto the stage.

Vicky had worried ahead of time about the quality of the rooms, since they had been so cheap. Turin is not a major tourist destination, so it doesn't have a lot of the standard tourist infrastructure one would find in, say, Nice. There are not many apartments to rent for short stays. Of the few she had found, these two had the best location, so she went with them, but with little confidence. Vicky had also worried about the fact that the rooms didn't connect, which meant that the kids would be on their own. But we're at the end of a quiet hall, with just a few steps between the two rooms, so that's fine. And though the rooms themselves are plain and simple, they are perfectly adequate.

The best features of the apartments are the balcony doors that open onto the courtyard. The balconies themselves are barely broad enough to stand on. But the courtyard has elegant stone decorations here and there and is filled at all hours with swallows darting and wheeling. For the next few nights, I will lie awake in the heat, balcony doors wide open, and watch their sleek black silhouettes above the courtyard's gabled roof against the glowing air of the city.

But not yet. First we have to move in, then we have to buy supplies for tomorrow's meals, since it will be the Sabbath and we don't want to spend money in restaurants. This is part of the reason we sought our own apartments—so we would have a refrigerator and space to make our own meals.

Finding a grocery is tricky, though. By now it's after six and most stores are closed. Maria sings us an aria by Verdi about a supermarket being around the corner and down the street—from one of his lesser-known works, *Aïda en Supermerchado*—and we manage to find it.

It's here that the remainder of my energy dissipates and I really start to fade. Shopping in a strange market is challenging enough, but doing it late on a hot day, a travel day, with five other people, puts me over the edge. Too hot, too tired, too not-at-home in my surroundings. My head is down, my replies are curt or nonexistent, and if I have to deal with the children I'm going to snap at them.

Vicky, however, feels fine. In the market, she manages the competing desires for different foods among the six of us well, ensuring there is enough to see us through three meals but not too much duplicate shopping. And while I'm sinking into fatigue and becoming monosyllabic, Vicky is bubbling with excitement about the new place, the new streets, the new sights, and her energy carries the children with her.

Marriage is a binary system. If the two of you are in different moods, with one doing well and the other not, you wind up averaging out. The downside of this arrangement is that the one in a good mood is slowed by the one in a bad mood; the upside is that the one not doing well is buoyed by the other. So there we are: I'm exhausted, oppressed by the heat and frustrated by my inability to speak Italian, while Vicky feels great, exhilarated to be in a country she's never visited before and beginning to fall in love with Turin.

Nietzsche's situation was different, of course. When he sank into himself, from being sick or lonely or discouraged, he sank without a lifeguard nearby to haul him back up. He knew this—he defines a friend as a "cork" that keeps "the hermit ... from sinking into the depths"[109]—but for most of the days of his life he was at a loss for such a friend. On the other hand, when he was in a bright mood he didn't have to commiserate with someone else's darker moods and be dragged down. When he was on a productive tear, he could ride the wave for hours, days, weeks, without anyone interrupting his thoughts. But a binary system can fly too, when both people are doing well. Two people in sync can reach higher emotional heights than one, can spark each other's thoughts, can provide perspective for one another.

"A married philosopher," writes Nietzsche, "belongs *in comedy*."[110] But he has no idea what he's talking about. And since my marriage is such a huge factor in my life, it's one respect in which I feel quite estranged from Nietzsche.

109   Z I.14
110   GM III.7

Shabbat – *chiuso per restauro*

IN HIS LATER writings, Nietzsche blasts the concept of a Sabbath. He says the point of the Sabbath is to be so boring that you lust for a return to work[111], or again that "those who suffer from the impoverishment of life ... seek rest, stillness, calm seas."[112] Those who are truly strong, by contrast, revel in continual struggle.

But this doesn't at all apply to Shabbat as I know it. The Jewish Sabbath (and I bet this is true of other religious traditions that have a formal day of rest) is not a mere absence of work. Rather, via a combination of religious requirements and traditional customs, the rest that takes place on that day becomes a positive and active engagement as opposed to a withdrawal from the world. Going to synagogue, or spending time with family, or having special meals, or enjoying nature, or reading things you don't have time for during the week, or even just sitting and contemplating one's life, or nature, or nothing at all, are all activities that give the day a positive and cherished content. The description of Shabbat that comes in the fourth commandment (in the Deuteronomy version) includes the note that God rested on the seventh day *vayinafash*, which means literally, "and was re-souled." And that's just how I think of it for myself—it's the day I recover

111   BGE 189
112   GS 370

my sense of self, my inner balance.

Nietzsche does seem to understand this idea in terms of place:

> *Country sensibility* —If a man has not drawn firm, restful lines along the horizon of his life, like the lines drawn by mountain and forest, his innermost will itself grows restless, distracted, and covetous, as is the nature of the city-dweller....[113]

But he doesn't recognize that this applies to time just as much, or even more. This blindness is even more striking in combination with the epigram immediately preceding the one I just quoted:

> *Value of illness*—The man who lies ill in bed sometimes discovers that what he is ill from is usually his office, his business or his society and that through them he has lost all circumspection with regard to himself: he acquires this wisdom from the leisure to which his illness has compelled him.[114]

Illnesses come when we need them, he seems to be saying (long before the invention of the word "psychosomatic"), so that we have surcease from activity that is keeping us from connecting with our true selves. There might well be something to that. But what Nietzsche doesn't get is that this is exactly the function of Shabbat, only rather than wait for ourselves to get sick, we program that re-souling time into our lives on a regular basis, every week. Maybe Nietzsche

---

113   HAH 290
114   HAH 289

wouldn't have gotten so sick so often, wouldn't have had his catastrophic breakdown, if he had had regular, positive, deliberately chosen rests rather than having his only times of rest be the result of illnesses that forced rest upon him. In other words, perhaps he wouldn't have broken down so young if he had observed Shabbat. I'm quite serious about this.

The other thing Nietzsche totally misses about having a regularly scheduled rest day is that it allows one to share that day with others. If we were to all take individual days of rest, just when *we* need them, our days might never line up with anyone else's. But a common day of rest allows for shared time. It disrupts our own productive rhythms, sure, but what we're doing is sacrificing some individuality for the sake of life with others. And maybe there's a different sort of individuality to be had in that way, an individuality that, rather than requiring isolation, includes connection with others.

I'm referring to family here of course, but a religious tradition creates a "family" in a larger sense, too. Here's another aspect of religion that Nietzsche and I disagree on: the appeal of being part of a religious tradition whose practitioners live all over the planet, so that a traveler from anywhere in the world may drop in at a synagogue anywhere in the world and both know what's going on and be welcomed like a long-lost relative (which, given the history and limited numbers of the Jewish people, one can say without too much exaggeration the traveler probably actually is).

Nietzsche certainly had sufficient exposure to the idea of a transnational community. The Lutheran church in which his father was a pastor and to which his mother remained piously devoted had spread worldwide already in his day. He had access to such a tradition if he wanted it. For me, this is a strong part of the appeal of Judaism, in which I and my wife were raised, as well as my parents before me and my children after me. There are far fewer Jews than Lutherans, but we also can be found all over the world.

Perhaps Nietzsche found this oppressive. Perhaps the very prominence of Lutheranism in Germany (where it is the majority Christian denomination) made it repugnant to him, yet another thing he fled from, whereas the smaller numbers of Jews (who are a minority most places in the world) make finding a fellow underdog a rarer and more precious event, one which doesn't diminish one's individuality. Indeed today, with so many Jews leaving the fold, as well as people raised in other traditions, one could make the case that holding on to one's religion could potentially be a positive expression of individuality, not conformism, if done for the right reasons.

Walking down Via Carlo Alberto from our apartment to the *sinagogo*, we see across the street a man with a *kippah* on his head walking in the same direction as us. He notices us too, and across the street we wish each other *shabbat shalom*.

I love the instant recognition and the instant fellowship. We've never met him before, but we know where he's going, and he knows where we're going, and it's the same place. I guess I can understand why Nietzsche might turn away from this—he doesn't want to be known, doesn't want to be pinned to a group identity. "Above all, do not mistake me for someone else,"[115] he writes at the beginning of his autobiography, and I find this a very noble goal: to be unmistakably unique. But I don't mind part of me being recognized by others in this way. I know that part of me is not all of me, so I'm comfortable giving it its due. It's a connection to a fellow human, and it feels to me entirely positive, not at all constraining.

Yesterday it was marriage that distanced me from Nietzsche, today it's religious identity. It's strange how quickly

---

115   EH Preface.1

the fellowship I felt with him in Nice has dissipated here in Turin. It's as if we got on two different trains.

THE synagogue, Tempio Israelitico, is located on Piazzetta Primo Levi. Levi was a chemist and Jewish native of Turin best known for his account of his year in Auschwitz. The synagogue has four pale yellow Moorish turrets, giving it a very similar look to the synagogue in Florence, which I saw with my family twenty-five years ago. Perhaps Jewishness feels non-European to Italians, even to Italian Jews.

There is a police car across the street and an armed guard at the gate. There has been a spate of violence recently directed at European synagogues (so maybe our nervousness at the Jewish star on our apartment door wasn't so paranoid). Fortunately, the guard speaks Hebrew, so I don't need to rely on my pathetic Italian to convince him we're okay. Even so, he wants to know where in the US we're from before he'll let us in.

Inside, a greeter gestures us toward steps leading down to a chapel. The chapel is built out of some sort of dark wood and has steeply pitched seating and leather-lined pews. Its overall modern design is somewhat at odds with the ornate, antique reader's platform in the middle of the room and, at the eastern end, with the ornate, antique ark for the Torah scrolls. Seating is separate for men and women. The boys and I take prayer shawls from the rack outside and find places to sit on a pew facing Vicky and the girls.

Services are lovely. In some respects, they are global, for here in Turin we are reading the same Torah portion, with precisely the same Hebrew wording, as in other services being conducted all over the world at this very same time (well, with accommodation for different time zones)—another aspect of belonging to a global religion that I get a kick out of. In other respects these services resemble the Spanish-Portuguese style I grew up with[116], yet some of the tunes are Ashkenazic (i.e. from German/Eastern European traditions). And some tunes and practices are unique, for Italian Judaism is historically a third stream, intermediate between the Sephardic/Ashkenazic split that dominates Judaism as a whole, due to its antiquity: The Italian Jewish community goes back to Roman times and is thus one of the oldest in the world.

One of the most distinctive features of services at Tempio Israelitico is the vocal style. I've been to services in England and heard the influence of English choral harmonies on congregational singing there. Here in Italy, the cantor and rabbi show they know where they are by letting loose from time to time with some purely operatic vocals. I've never been very fond of operatic singing by cantors in the US, but here it seems authentic and appropriate.

As is common in most synagogues, when a guest is present he is given the honor of being called up to the Torah. It gives me pride to fulfill this function representing my family and I am proud too that my children know to stand while I am up on the platform—a custom of the Italian as well as the Sephardic synagogues. It's understood that such an honor is usually acknowledged with a donation and when we get back to the States I will send them a check, even though I know they will have a tough time cashing a check made out in dollars.

The sermon is delivered in Italian of course, but to my surprise I can follow some of it. The word *controverso* stands out—equivalent, I'm sure, to the Hebrew *makhloket*, a dispute

116   This, by the way, is a respect in which I am a minority even within American Judaism, and thus, I suppose, another reason why maintaining an ancient tradition actually feels to me like it accentuates my individuality rather than trammels it.

between Talmudic sages—but I don't understand enough of the rest to be able to reconstruct for you just what the dispute was.

Afterwards, there is *kiddush*—a short ceremony celebrating the Sabbath and involving wine and cakes or cookies—and we are greeted by many people. Three stand out: The rabbi turns out to be a friend of the current rabbi of my home synagogue in Philadelphia and has even visited there more recently than I. A congregant who speaks excellent English apologizes to us for the heat, saying it's "off warranty," which gives a good chuckle, since we're accustomed back home to saying that the weather in Maine is *always* unusual—either unusually hot, or cold, or wet, or dry—and it appears we've brought it with us to Turin.

The third person we meet is none other than Ariel Finzi. We blink. Of the Finzi-Continis, we ask? Yes, *that* Finzi, he acknowledges with a smile. A lovely man, he gives us a tour of the main sanctuary upstairs—a magnificent space that he says is burdened by poor acoustics and is, in any event, too large to be used on any but the most populated occasions, such as Yom Kippur or lifecycle events (this is typical of many American synagogues as well).

After the tour, Ariel says he would invite us to his home for lunch (all six of us, with no advance notice!); but it is eight kilometers away and he would not want to make us walk such a distance in this heat. As it happens, we are actually liberal enough to ride on Shabbat for such purposes (observant Jews do not ride in motorized vehicles on the Sabbath), but Ariel clearly is not. The devotion he shows in walking five miles in this heat to get to synagogue, and then another five back, still impresses me. We thank him, but are happy to return to our apartment, stocked with food from yesterday's late grocery trip.

We walk home thoroughly satisfied with our excursion into the world of Judaism, Torino branch. We were able to recognize and fit in with and participate in customs both ancient and global, and were shown hospitality simply for walking through the door and identifying with that heritage. Less than twenty-four hours in this town and we were able to speak with natives as if we were long-lost friends. Nietzsche lived here for months and knew hardly anyone other than his landlord.

Homeward for our lunch and our nap—one of the most important modes of Shabbat worship, in my book. Besides, we need our rest, for in the evening we will meet Nietzsche's ghost.

Morality & Flogging Horses

AFTER NAPS and a snack of yogurt, cheese and fruit, we head down Via Cavour towards the river. We pass through the Piazza Cavour, a lovely little park with surprising, mid-city hillocks—Turin is otherwise essentially flat. At the river we turn left and are now, strolling along the Lungo Po, once again in Nietzsche's footsteps. The parks along the banks of the river Po were his favorite good-weather walking routes in Turin; in the rain he stayed under the arcades.

We come to the Ponte Vittorio Emanuele I and walk a few steps out over the river to the middle of the bridge. Before us, dramatically situated at the head of the bridge across from the city, is the 19th century Gran Madre di Dio church, radiating power via the six neoclassical pillars arrayed across its elaborate façade. To our left and our right are parklands, stretching as far as the eye can see on both sides of the river. High up on a hill to the left, far off in the haze, the 18th century Basilica of Superga, its tall dome flanked by towers and fronted by more pillars, dominates the horizon at the eastern edge of the city. Behind us is the Via Po, lined up with the bridge and the church, leading straight to the historic city center.

Nietzsche wrote about this very spot in his first letter from Turin, when he had recovered his spirits after his train disaster at Sampierdarena and was beginning to feel like himself again:

> This is the city I can use *now*! That is
> crystal clear to me, and it was so from the
> very first moment…. [F]or the feet as well
> as the eyes it is a classic spot! What safety,
> what sidewalks, …[w]hat earnest and solemn
> piazzas! And the palaces are built without
> pretension, the streets clean and well
> made—everything far more dignified than I
> expected! …These arcades are necessary here,
> given the changeable weather: yet they are
> spacious, not at all oppressive. Evenings on
> the bridge over the Po: splendid! Beyond
> good and evil!![117]

That last phrase might seem an odd one to exclaim on
a bridge at twilight. Nietzsche clearly thinks the friend
receiving this letter will understand his meaning; for the rest
of us, though, some explanation is in order.

The phrase, one of Nietzsche's most notorious and the
title of the book published three years earlier for which he
was called "dynamite," appears to discard morality entirely.
And it's true that Nietzsche does in that book, and elsewhere,
call himself an "immoralist."[118] However, the matter is not so
simple. In a late section of *Beyond Good and Evil*, Nietzsche
proposes a contrast between the word pair "good/evil" and
the word pair "good/bad." The former, he says, connotes the
bitter reaction of oppressed slaves against their masters – they
defined "evil" as whatever was true of their masters' cruel
exercise of power, and then defined "good" as whatever was
opposite to this: humility, gentleness, etc. Nietzsche identifies

---

117   Letter to Peter Gast, April 7, 1888, in Krell & Bates 203
118   BGE 226. He's playing off the French term *moralistes*, the self-description of
a set of 18th C writers whose epigrammatic style and iconoclastic views Nietzsche
imitated in his middle works.

this way of determining moral value as the source of our contemporary morality and criticizes it for being reactive in that it defines evil first and only then defines good as what contrasts with it. The word pair "good/bad" on the other hand, as Nietzsche hears it, does not have this moralistic connotation. It connotes simply the way in which humans distinguish those things which enhance their lives from those which don't. This form of valuing is positive and creative, not negative and reactive.[119] We cannot live without valuing in this way, he thinks, and part of his point in giving this analysis is to move us beyond the *ressentiment* implicit in the word pair "good/evil" and on to the more naturalistic "good/bad."[120] The latter pair is the one that fits better with his overall project of promoting creative individualism.

However, there's a second aspect to Nietzsche's criticism of contemporary morality, and it's actually this second sense of the phrase "beyond good and evil" which I think is on Nietzsche's mind as he revels in the glory of twilight on the bridge over the river Po. Our contemporary morality, since it establishes standards of self-effacement and purity which we can never live up to, inevitably leads us to condemn the world. If we hold moral values to be the highest ones there are, we will inevitably be unable to affirm the value of life. We will condemn this life as unworthy and will pine for an impossibly perfect afterlife rather than work to make this life affirmable. For this reason, Nietzsche sometimes calls morality "anti-life."[121]

Does Nietzsche then want us to *be* evil? He is sometimes taken that way, but this is definitely a misinterpretation.

---

119   BGE 260
120   This analysis is developed at much greater length in GM I.
121   One place he does this is in the "Attempt at a Self-Criticism" that was added to BT as a preface when its second edition was issued in 1886 (see section 5). Since this piece was written right after BGE, I feel justified in taking the one to gloss the other.

The good/bad word pair is sufficient to maintain moral standards—truth-telling is good, lying is bad; courage is good, cowardice is bad, etc.—and in fact right in the middle of *Beyond Good and Evil* Nietzsche lists virtue as one of the things "for whose sake it is worthwhile to live on earth."[122] So the phrase "beyond good and evil" means, in this second sense, that we should look beyond moral valuations to find the value of life.

So what might there be beyond morality that can justify life? "Whatever is done from love always occurs beyond good and evil."[123] And what does Nietzsche love above all else? The answer is easy—art, in all its forms. In his very first book, he declares, "it is only as an *aesthetic phenomenon* that existence and the world are eternally *justified*."[124] Judging the world by moral standards alone will lead us to condemn the world, since neither we nor the world can ever live up to those standards. But aesthetic beauty, Nietzsche believes, puts ordinary moral considerations into perspective. Morality should blend with the enjoyment of life, not conflict with it. And it is aesthetic high points—not just human-made artworks but also the beauty of nature, beautiful sunsets, etc.—which can be affirmed as sufficient to justify life.

Having been there myself, I can now, along with Nietzsche, attest to the life-affirming power of the splendid, 360-degree view from the bridge over the river Po at sunset.

AFTER a few moments of affirmation, we turn back from the bridge and start walking up the Via Po towards the city center. The first few blocks are an open mall, the Piazza

122   BGE 188
123   BGE 153
124   BT 5

Vittorio Veneto. Then the street's upper blocks resume the usual Turinese pattern of stores under covered arcades. As we get further from the bridge, the street feels narrower as the stores crowd closer to it under the arcades. And suddenly I remember that this is where Nietzsche lost his mind.

Or at least was said to have lost his mind. When I was a student, and for many years after, all the biographies of Nietzsche told a similar story: On the morning of January 3rd, 1889, Nietzsche, out for his customary walk, came upon a coachman whipping a horse which had fallen. Something in the scene caused Nietzsche to snap. He ran over to the horse and threw his arms around its neck, sobbing uncontrollably, and was from then on, for the remaining eleven and a half years of his physical life, an empty shell of himself. The extraordinary pathos of this story, including the implication that what broke him was the stupid small-mindedness of humanity—an undeniably Nietzschean theme[125]—has made it famous even among those who know little else about Nietzsche.

The only problem with this story is that it is probably not true. Recent scholarship (of which I confess I was not aware when I walked on the Via Po) has failed to turn up any written account of the incident till after Nietzsche's death in 1900, and even then only in an anonymous article in an Italian tabloid from which one would not expect much journalistic accuracy even if there were a byline. And then the most lurid, most memorable accounts of the story date from much later, after World War II.[126] So it is likely that the story has been greatly embellished, if indeed there is any truth to it at all.

---

125   See, for example, Z Prologue.5.
126   See Verrecchia A. "Nietzsche's Breakdown in Turin." in Harrison T, ed. *Nietzsche in Italy.* Saratoga: Stanford University Press, 1988: 105–12. My thanks to Emery Moreira for bringing this article to my attention.

What is clear is that on or about that date, Nietzsche experienced some sort of catastrophic breakdown. His letters before then are as copious as ever and entirely coherent; his letters afterwards are neither. The post-breakdown letters have been recovered and can be found in Walter Kaufmann's *The Portable Nietzsche*.[127] They are both fascinating and heartbreaking. It is as if Nietzsche's mind had been dashed to the ground and broken open. All the pieces of his mind are there, but they are in complete disarray. Here is the letter to his friend Peter Gast, entire:

> Turin, January 4, 1889
> To my maestro Pietro,
> Sing me a new song: the world is transfigured and all the heavens are full of joy.
> The Crucified

Another letter is addressed to an old colleague from the University of Basel named Jakob Burckhardt. It is dated January 6th despite having been posted in Turin on the 5th. It is long and, in some parts, reasonable. For example, Nietzsche reports "I have reserved myself a small student's room, situated opposite the Palazzo Carignano…which also permits me to hear from the desk the magnificent music below, in the Galleria Subalpina." This is all correct. But in the middle, where I put an ellipsis, he writes "(in which I was born as Vittorio Emanuele)." At other points in the letter he claims to be other people; Prado, father Prado, Lesseps (I don't know who the first two are, but Lesseps was the architect of the Suez Canal—his attempt to build a canal in Panama had just gone bankrupt in December 1888), Chambige (also unknown to

---

127   See pages 685-687.

me), Count Robilant (a Turinese native and Italian statesman who had just died in October), Carlo Alberto (Savoy king during the Italians' first stab at independence in 1848—this is the name of the street that runs from the Piazza Carignano, where Nietzsche's residence at the time is located, to our apartment), and Antonelli (the architect of the Mole Antonelliana, which we will visit on Monday)—and then says finally, "at bottom I am every name in history." In a postscript he refers to Cosima Wagner as Ariadne.

And here is the final letter, addressed to another old Basel colleague, Franz Overbeck, in its entirety:

> January 6, 1889
> To friend Overbeck and wife. Although you have so far demonstrated little faith in my ability to pay, I yet hope to demonstrate that I am somebody who pays his debts—for example, to you. I am just having all anti-Semites shot.
> Dionysus

Note the opposition to anti-Semitism and the positive connotation for the universal moral value of paying one's debts—both genuine parts of Nietzsche's worldview, despite his reputation—and the identification with Dionysus, the Greek god of wine, whose ancient festival of wild ecstasy was an important symbol for Nietzsche. *Ecce Homo* ends with the line, "Have I been understood? Dionysus versus the Crucified!"[128] His meaning seems to be that we must overcome the nihilism about this world implied by Christian otherworldliness and instead embrace this life ecstatically in all its contradictions. In this letter he has become Dionysus,

---

128   EH destiny.9

though in the letter to Gast he was the Crucified. Again, he seems to be every name in history.

At the time of his breakdown Nietzsche was boarding with the Fino family on the top floor of the Galleria Subalpina. The Finos could not have known the content of these letters, but they could see for themselves from Nietzsche's behavior during the days after January 3rd that something was wrong with him. He would have long crying jags. He sometimes twitched and spoke incomprehensible nonsense. Signora Fino, at one point hearing a ruckus in his room, through the keyhole spied him prancing about naked and erect, singing something unrecognizable.

Contacted by the Finos, who found their addresses on letters in Nietzsche's room, Burckhardt and Overbeck came to Turin to collect their broken friend and bring him to a sanatorium in Switzerland. After a few days his mother arrived and took him back to Germany, first to another sanatorium and then home to Naumburg. He eventually stopped speaking entirely, although he continued to be physically healthy and to eat heartily. His mother would take him for walks around Naumburg, believing that fresh air would restore his sanity, but his bizarre behavior and incomprehensible linguistic outbursts were so embarrassing that she had to take him far out of town to avoid meeting up with anyone, and eventually she gave up. His sister, Elisabeth, after suing her mother for custody of Nietzsche and his literary legacy, set him up in a house in Weimar.[129] From this base she worked to spread his fame. She would dress him in a robe and laurel wreath and invite the intellectuals of the day to commune with him, for although he had been fairly obscure for most of his creative career, he was now, ironically, after his collapse and thanks

129   The house is open for touring. For many years the Nietzsche Archive, which is also in Weimar, was located there; it is now stored at and administered by the Goethe-Schiller Archive.

to the attention afforded by Brandes and others, becoming famous. The visitors would sit across from him in the salon, while Elisabeth intoned, "He is thinking across the centuries, beyond humanity," putting an absurd face on his catatonia. He lived in that pathetic condition for eleven years, a full fifth of his physical lifetime, before dying on August 25, 1900. But his life really ended on or about January 3rd, 1889, somewhere in the vicinity of the Via Po.

We are now walking on that very street, and I, still believing the old story of the horse, am looking for signs of where that exact spot may have been. Some accounts say the collapse happened in the Via Po, others that it was a street just off the Via Po, and I now see how both descriptions could work: The arcades that line the Via Po cover the side streets as they cross, so that one could be walking under a Via Po arcade and yet be on the pavement of one of the side streets. But the precise spot of the breakdown, if it in fact occurred, was not recorded. Was it Via delle Rosine? Via Montebello? Via San Massimo? Via Rossini? Via Vasco? Via San Francesco da Paola? Via Bogino? Via Carlo Alberto? If the story is true, it *has* to be one of those eight. By the time we reach the end of Via Po, I am gripped powerfully by the melancholy thought that we have just walked past the spot where the great Nietzsche supposedly lost his mind.

No one around me seems to be gripped by that thought, though. My family is window shopping and so are the Turinese, more and more of them. The street gradually fills with the Saturday evening *passagiero*—a meet-and-greet stroll practiced on most evenings in most Italian towns. When the sky is finally dark, the night's fun of restaurants, music, and shows will get into full swing. Somehow, life has managed to go on without Nietzsche.

WE get to the head of the Via Po and turn left, beginning a clockwise circuit of the Piazza Castello, the historic center of Turin. There are shops here on both sides of the arcade, so the passageway for walking is crowded and dark. Not quite sure where we're going, we step through a gateway and find ourselves in a large, four-story atrium filled with café chairs and tables. The floor level is all shops; halfway up is an ornamental balcony. The ceiling is a giant skylight held up by a 19th century iron framework. For some reason this scene looks vaguely familiar and suddenly I realize we're standing in Nietzsche's house.

This is the Galleria Subalpina—I have recognized it from the photograph in *The Good European*. How could we have wandered in unknowingly? I finally realize that even though Nietzsche's address was 6 Via Carlo Alberto and even though the descriptions of Nietzsche's room that I've read all mention that it faced the Piazza Carignano, the Galleria Subalpina is so big that it extends from that *piazza* all the way to the next *piazza*, the Piazza Castello, which is where we were just walking. So we have stepped into it from the rear. And the passage went unremarked because the gate to the atrium through which we just entered reads not Galleria Subalpina but Café Romano, which must be the name of one of the two cafés that do business here.

I get goosebumps when I realize where we are and I want to stay and soak it in more. But Vicky points out that it is getting late. She assures me we'll come back another day, a day when we have our cameras and also have more time and energy to explore. We step out the way we came in, from the Galleria into the arcade at the southwest corner of the

Piazza Castello, most likely the same direction Nietzsche would have taken out that same gate, into that same arcade, heading towards the Via Po, embarking on the walk where, supposedly, he would give up his mind.

And suddenly I feel inside what it was like to be him; writing, writing until his eyes watered and his back ached and his hand cramped, rushing down the stairs and then outside to take a break. Thoughts coming too fast, thoughts *of the revaluation of all values, of the task I must place upon humanity, to which most will not be equal, a task to cultivate humanity*, too many thoughts, too fast....

All these phrases from his writings of those last few months in Turin,[130] that I'm sure were tumbling all together in his head in an unbearable crescendo as he neared his crisis, now tumble through my head as I think of him heading out this very gate on January 3rd, 1889. No one knows where he took his final walk, or what, if anything, happened that triggered his breakdown. It's a relief, then, to be able to tell you with certainty that I and my family turned left, away from the Via Po, walked partway around the Piazza Castello and then back along the Via Roma to our apartment.

---

130   Versions of all of these phrases can be found in the Prefaces to T, A, and EH, as well as in notebook passages from 1888.

Nobility & the Last Man

THE 20TH OF SEPTEMBER, 1870, was when the final step in Italian unification took place. Italian troops entered Rome, ending the Pope's temporal authority and making Rome Italy's capital. This marked the first time since the end of the Roman Empire that the entire Italian peninsula constituted a single political entity. That entity was ruled by Turin's own Victor Emmanuel II, of the House of Savoy, and today we have come to the Via XX Settembre to catch the bus to Veneria Reale, the recently restored historic royal seat of the House of Savoy.

Sunday mornings are quiet in pretty much every Christian-majority locale, and Turin is no exception. It's a little spooky, what with the streets almost entirely empty and long rows of heavy-set buildings glowering down at us. Being tourists is nerve-racking enough without having a bunch of hulking, over-muscled buildings looming over you like they're about to mug an innocent family of six. And of course, after our Èzé adventure I'm a little nervous about buses.

But the bus does come, and it's the right one. We board successfully and we're on our way—past more imposing buildings, then a charming park, then the Porta Susa train station, just as old and picturesque as Porta Nuova but now used only for commuters. Once we leave the historic center though, the outskirts of Turin look much like outskirts anywhere—gas stations, strip malls and so forth. Veneria Reale was at one time way out in the country, but it is now just an outpost in modern-day Torino's urban sprawl. This homogenization of the modern urban landscape would surely have saddened Nietzsche, who celebrated a cosmopolitan Europe in which the variety of idiosyncratic cultures—and, presumably, architectural styles— would be maintained.

The House of Savoy is less famous than the House of Tudor, or the Bourbon dynasty, or the Romanovs, but none of these lasted as long. Its first scion, Humbert I, became, in the year 1003, the Count of Sabaudia (from which the name "Savoy" evolved). In 1416 Amadeus VII was elevated by the Holy Roman Emperor to the rank of Duke of Savoy, and in 1713 Charles Emmanuel II was rewarded for his loyalty to the Hapsburgs by being granted the title of King of Sardinia. You can see already the patient persistence of the line, waiting three or four centuries each time until they get their next promotion.

It was as King of Sardinia that Victor Emmanuel II was put forward by 19th century nationalists as a potential unifier for Italy as a whole. According to legend, the success of the opera composer Giuseppe Verdi furthered the *Risorgimento* by providing a convenient acronym—nationalists could shout "Viva Verdi!" and mean "*Viva Victor Emmanuel Re D'Italia*". And sure enough, Victor Emmanuel became King of Italy in 1861. The title was a bit ahead of itself—Venice and Rome had yet to sign on for reunification. But the fact that Rome was not yet part of reunified Italy made way for Turin to be modern Italy's first capital. The new nation declared itself as such in 1861 in the Teatro Carignano, right across the street from what would twenty-seven years later be the window of Nietzsche's apartment. September 20, 1870, then, marking the inclusion of Rome and the culmination of the *Risorgimento*, was the Savoy dynasty's high point, making the fact that we boarded the bus to Veneria Reale on Via XX Settembre quite appropriate.

After such a long ascent, the Savoyards' low point followed quite quickly—just a couple of generations later. In the year 1922, despite advice from his generals that a lowlife thug and his ragtag band of right-wing lunatics should be eliminated, Victor Emmanuel III instead turned around and appointed Benito Mussolini prime minister, allowing him to spearhead the rise of Fascism in Italy well before either Franco or Hitler could get going in their respective countries. This policy came a cropper, of course, in World War II. Italy's involvement in the war was an unmitigated disaster for all concerned: first for the Italians, who wound up with their beautiful country in tatters; then for the Germans, who, after Mussolini was finally deposed in 1943, had to post troops to cover yet another front; and finally for the Italian Jews, who had survived the war pretty well until that point. Italians were generally not anti-Semitic, even *i fascisti*, and they did not collaborate with the Nazis to the extent that many other European nations did—but now Italian Jews were prey to the German SS. By the end of the war some eight thousand had perished, including several of Ariel Finzi's relatives. For this involvement with Mussolini (and in the generally democratic spirit of the post-war period all over the world), Italians voted in 1946 to end the monarchy altogether.

The House of Savoy was sent to pasture then, with a tally of nine and a half centuries of rule, far longer than any other European royal house. Even their end was relatively benign— no guillotine or bloody *coup d'etat*, just a plebiscite. Although, to be sure, the end wasn't entirely friendly: The Italian constitution, enacted in 1947, included a specific provision that expressly barred males of the Savoy line from so much as entering the country. This draconian provision was not rescinded until 2002 and even so, it was only at the price of the last Victor Emmanuel explicitly renouncing his claim to the throne. *Sic transit gloria*, as the Italians' Roman ancestors used to say—thus passes glory, eventually, even for the long-lasting Savoys.

The Savoy kings never ruled an area as big as, say, the House of Windsor or the Ch'ing dynasty, but they did, bit by bit—acquiring a city here, making an advantageous marriage there—gradually build themselves a decent sized country in what is now northwestern Italy, southeastern France and some neighbouring islands. Using the fertility of the Piedmont and the strategic location of the Riviera as their geopolitical capital, they were both prosperous and powerful, and were significant players in European politics for centuries.

And their bailiwick is precisely the territory we're traveling in. In a sense, our entire two-week trip could be billed as a tour of the Savoys' estate, and it's nice that we're finally getting to visit the manor house.

Nietzsche spent a good amount of time in Savoyland, not just Nice and Turin but several other towns in the vicinity as well, such as Rapallo and Genoa. When he finally made a home for himself in Turin, he placed himself right in the Savoy capital, across the street from the Teatro Carignano and just a couple hundred meters from the Palazzo Reale. Was this mere coincidence, or did it connect with his lifelong fixation on nobility? The letter I quoted in the previous chapter about the beauty of evenings on the bridge over the river Po includes excitement about the aristocratic feel of Turin:

> What a worthy and serious city! Not at all a metropolis, not at all modern, as I had feared: rather, it is a city of seventeenth-century royalty, which has but one commanding taste in all things, that of the court and the nobles....

Many people who enjoy other aspects of Nietzsche's philosophy—perspectivism, individualism, the eternal recurrence, etc.—find his fixation on nobility worrisome. On the one hand, many of the nobles he talks about in his writing were brutal killers: the Borgia family, Frederick the Great, Napoleon, etc. And on the other hand, his praise of aristocracy and criticisms of democracy cut against the grain of our time even more than in his. At one point he even says slavery is necessary for higher culture.

We may wish to consider why Nietzsche held this position. Here's that line about slavery in its full context:

> Every enhancement of the type 'man' has so far been the work of an aristocratic society ... a society that believes in the long ladder of an order of rank and differences in value between man and man, and that needs slavery in some sense or other. Without that *pathos of distance* which grows out of the ingrained difference between strata ... that other, more mysterious pathos could not have grown up either —the craving for an ever new widening of distances within soul itself, the development of ever higher, rarer, more remote, further-stretching, more comprehensive states—in brief, simply the enhancement of the type 'man,' the continual 'self-overcoming of man,' to use a moral formula in a supra-moral sense.[131]

The idea that hierarchy in society is mirrored by hierarchy in the individual soul goes back at least to Plato's *Republic*. Whereas Plato envisions both the ideal society and the ideal

---

131   BGE 257

individual soul as existing in some sort of static harmony, Nietzsche sees them both as dynamic. Just as leadership in society—political, artistic, intellectual—spurs the whole society to move forward, leadership in the soul (that is, some parts being stronger or more valued than others) provides a push for the individual to change and grow. Improvement requires comparison and comparison requires difference, and thus both societal and individual cultural progress require inequality of some sort or other. This is a provocative hypothesis, but not an entirely crazy one. I read Nietzsche's use of the word "slavery" here as a bit of hyperbole in keeping with his overall rhetorical strategy of deliberate provocation (somewhat in the same vein as our current phrase, "wage slavery").

The second thing to note is that Nietzsche's ultimate aim is to define nobility of *character*. The part of *Beyond Good and Evil* that the quoted passage comes from is entitled "What is Noble," and I think it is fair to say that the connection of nobility of character with nobility in the sense of inherited aristocracy is not a mere homonym. Ideally, being noble includes a strong conscious sense of one's own identity, of pride in one's personal history and active capabilities, which do indeed seem to be good things to have. Nietzsche lists other qualities which seem appropriate for a philosophy of individualism:

> Signs of nobility: never thinking of degrading our duties into duties for everybody; not wanting to delegate, to share, one's own responsibility; counting one's privileges and their exercise among one's *duties*.[132]

---

132   BGE 272

These are all noble things, I think we'd agree. A little later he writes, "The noble soul has reverence for itself,"[133] and I like that line too, understanding "reverence" to connote self-respect rather than egotism. Elsewhere, Nietzsche develops the notion of personal sovereignty, noting that being a sovereign individual, "a creature with the right to make promises," is one of the triumphs of human development.[134] In light of all this, it's not unreasonable for him, I think, to study nobility of character, or to make conceptual points about what it is like to exercise sovereignty over oneself, by considering historical nobles and actual sovereigns.

Nor is Nietzsche alone in doing so: People at the upper echelon of society have always fascinated all of us, whether or not their characters are noble and deserving of our consideration. Consider how many books, plays, movies and television series concern aristocrats, far out of proportion to their actual percentage of the world's population. I have always thought this is because the aristocrats are the ones who have full autonomy (or at least appear to at first glance). They have the money or the political power or the license to live in full control of themselves, unlike their servants, who live under significant constraints. Thus, they work better as literary figures—they have freedom of motion and so can be the subjects of stories (even when those stories ultimately are about discovering limits to their power). In the Talmud, for example, illustrative parables are often introduced with the line, "It's like with a king…" even if the person in the parable is not a king and what he is doing has nothing to do with crown-wearing or ruling or anything of the sort. Thus, part of Nietzsche's focus on nobility comes simply from the need to describe sovereign people who can then serve as examples

133   BGE 287
134   GM II.1

for the rest of us in whatever respects we find ourselves free.

In addition, while the Borgias and their ilk may not have had admirable characters—and Nietzsche never denies this—it has to be admitted that they got things done, and often some very worthwhile things: The Borgias were great patrons of the arts, Napoleon modernized Europe, and so forth. Nietzsche worries that our emphasis on equality and our concern for the downtrodden keep us from getting things done in the pursuit of excellence, innovation, and cultural/ spiritual growth. As we saw back in Nice, the fact that Nietzsche's residence on Rue de Ponchettes was swallowed up by a restaurant on the Cours Saleya illustrates nicely the idea that for something to grow, something else must be subsumed; for something new to be created, something else must be destroyed; for something to be found excellent, something else must be considered mediocre. These may be harsh truths, but Nietzsche doesn't care who he offends. His argument that the leveling tendency of democracy is bad for the higher man is at least cautionary.[135] Nietzsche expresses admiration for those who sacrifice other considerations to their own ambition because he believes that's what it takes for ambition to bear fruit.

Here's where I disagree, however: It seems to me that the pursuit of artistic and intellectual creativity does not require ruthlessly subsuming others to one's ambition. At least I sure hope not. Partly, I admit, this is simply a hope—I hope that by trying to do right by the people in my life, I haven't lost

---

135   Is Nietzsche being too Eurocentric here? That is, is his conception of democracy as the triumph of the rabble over the nobles (think of the French Revolution) in fact superseded by the American model, in which it is self-made democrats such as Benjamin Franklin who are the new nobility? Possibly, and I'll have more to say about Nietzsche's criticisms of democracy later. Still, in the context of this discussion of nobility, Nietzsche's fear of the levelling tendencies of democracy seems to me something to watch out for, at least in a cautionary way. Fans of Kurt Vonnegut will be reminded of this lesson in the short story, "Harrison Bergeron."

out on the opportunity to be the creative individual I've always been capable of being. I can imagine a case being made that people who want to be artistic or intellectual stars shouldn't have families in the first place, so that their energy and attention can remain focused on their work. However, I feel quite sure that once one has a family, they have to come first. Some might propose as a counter-example Gauguin abandoning his family to run away to Tahiti to develop his painting. But it seems quite clear to me that while Gauguin's art may be beautiful, his character is not.[136] Those who, like Cesare Borgia, *et al*, pursued their goals in murderous ways are not truly noble in my view. Perhaps Nietzsche, that sickly, unread, friendless, jobless disability pensioner, admired these individuals for the power he himself did not have. But I don't.

AFTER touring the palace—much of it still *chiuso per restauro*—we head down the street that runs from the palace gate straight into the town itself. At what feels like the center of town there's a *piazza* that looks like a time capsule, plain and simple—a little bubble of 18th century preserved amidst the urban sprawl. Indeed, far off, at the other end of the street from the palace, we can see that the street opens to a modern road. But here the architecture is preserved, and it actually feels more authentically old than the carefully restored palace. Maybe the best way to keep a place restored is simply to keep living there. The Savoys couldn't do it, but the people of the town of Veneria Reale have somehow pulled it off. The commoners have outlasted the royalty.

Not that this is something to be proud of, necessarily. In the preface to *Zarathustra*, Nietzsche excoriates "the last

---

136   For more on the Gauguin example, see Bernard Williams' *Moral Luck*.

man," who has, by aiming low and playing it safe, simply survived.[137] The fact that the last man has outlasted those who have dared much and perished in the process is not at all praiseworthy. After all, the coward who hides from a battle outlives the courageous soldier who charges into a breach. All the same, coming from the Savoys' empty hallways into these still vibrant streets, I am struck by the contrast. I have always admired things that survive: old buildings still standing, old books still worth reading, old music that still moves the soul. It is hard to deny that there is a form of strength that consists in simply hanging in there. Nietzsche would say the Savoys' subjects outlasted their rulers simply by keeping their heads down—nothing to be proud of. Others may say they deserve our respect because they're still here and still have their identity. Perhaps there is something to admire in both rulers and subjects.

---

[137] Z Prologue.5

Will to Power in the Molé Tower

MONDAY'S first target is the Molé Antonelliana, the tallest building in Turin. Begun in 1863, the Molé was completed in 1889, the same year as the Eiffel Tower, as well as the year of Nietzsche's collapse (it occurs to me that the buildings were going up right as he was going down). It is named for the architect, Alessandro Antonelli. It was originally meant to be a synagogue, and I admit I have trouble imagining that the tallest building in a Diaspora city would be a synagogue. Tel Aviv or Jerusalem sure, although even there the synagogues are not the tallest buildings. In ancient Jerusalem, of course, the Temple was the dominant building, but synagogues are usually more low-key. I guess the Jewish community of Turin wanted to show that they weren't anybody's ghetto pushovers anymore, that they had *arrived*. Upscale American synagogues often betray the same motive.

At any rate, despite their ambitions, the Jewish community was not in fact able to raise enough money to match Antonelli's repeatedly enlarged designs. The planned height of the dome grew continually over the duration of the project—from 121 meters in the original design to 146 meters, then to 153 and finally to the 167 meters we gape at today. Meanwhile the Jewish community began to shrink after 1864 when the new Italian capital moved to Florence. The rest of the Turinese, though, wouldn't let the project die. The city authorities traded land with the Jewish community—the latter used their new acquisition to build the smaller, but perfectly lovely synagogue we were just in on Saturday—and kept building. Plans changed, money came and went, but eventually the building was completed just a few months after (and just two or three blocks away from where), one way or another, Nietzsche collapsed.

The Molé's footprint is a perfect square. Its elegant façade features Corinthian columns on every side. Then there are Doric columns at the base of the dome and then still more columns at the peak of the dome, surrounding the observation deck. The metal-paneled dome is squared-off and suits the building perfectly. Atop it all is a round pinnacle. Unlike the Eiffel Tower or more modern skyscrapers, the Molé connotes not just verticality but substantial horizontal strength as well.

The Molé is just half the height of the Eiffel Tower and its square design means it would fit right in with downtown New York City's modernist boxes. Standing where it does, in a city that otherwise doesn't rise very high, it is dramatically beautiful, a worthy symbol of the city. I can't be sure Nietzsche wrote the following passage with the Molé in mind, but I do know that he wrote it in Turin for *Twilight of the Idols* and that there's no other building remotely like it in Nice or Sils-Maria or any of Nietzsche's other residences. So I rather suspect he is thinking of Antonelli and the Molé when he says the following:

> The *architect* represents ... the great act
> of will, the will that moves mountains, the
> frenzy of the great will which aspires to art.
> The most powerful human beings have always
> inspired architects; the architect has always

been under the spell of power. His buildings are supposed to render pride visible, and the victory over gravity, the will to power. Architecture is a kind of eloquence of power in forms—now persuading, even flattering, now only commanding. The highest feeling of power and sureness finds expression in a *grand style*. The power which no longer needs any proof, which spurns pleasing, which does not answer lightly, which feels no witness near, which lives oblivious of all opposition to it, which reposes within itself, fatalistically, a law among laws—that speaks of itself as a grand style.[138]

Nietzsche's paragraph describes the Molé much better than mine does. Without mentioning columns and domes, he instead perfectly captures the state of soul of both the original designer and the current onlookers.

After touring the vast interior and riding a glass elevator up into the spire for sweeping views of the city, we leave the Molé, grab some lunch, and head back to the Via Po. There amidst the rows of shops we find part of the University of Turin. The university was founded in 1404 and is thus one of the oldest in the world. By the end of the 17th century, it was already fairly run down, so the inauguration of this particular building in 1720, under the direction of the Savoy ruler at the time, Victor Amadeus II, was quite an important event in its history. Victor knew his business, too. The courtyard is an elegant square of white, carved stone, with grand staircases in each of the four corners.

The Chamberlain biography of Nietzsche reports that several well-read Turinese recognized his presence in town,

138   T XI.11

among them a University of Turin professor of philosophy by the name of Pasquale Ercole (this is 1888, remember, as Nietzsche's star is just beginning to rise). Yet Nietzsche for the most part avoided contact with him or anyone else.[139] I find this a frustrating biographical detail. In November 1887, while still in Nice, Nietzsche wrote a letter to a childhood friend, Erwin Rohde, one of his most faithful correspondents, that ends with a heartbreaking line: "I now have forty-three years behind me, and I am just as much alone as I was as a child."[140] Yet here he is in April 1888 declining a potential partner for conversation. On one level, I can understand that for Nietzsche solitude had become habitual and that he recoiled from having to explain himself too often. Come the fall of 1888, he would be presenting his solitude as chosen: "[A]ssociation with people imposes no mean test on my patience.... My humanity is a constant self-overcoming.... I need solitude—which is to say, recovery, return to myself... ."[141] That's all perfectly understandable, but then why the complaint about his loneliness in the letter from 1887? The contrast loses him some of my sympathy.[142]

Eventually, we find our way back to the Galleria Subalpina, where we were last Saturday. This time we go all the way inside. The interior is spacious, gently lit by the light coming through the glass ceiling four stories above. Late 19th century grillwork lines the interior facing of each floor. The center of the gallery is filled with tables set out by a café; probably not the very same chairs Nietzsche sat on to read his newspaper

---

139   Chamberlain 25 and 103
140   Letter of November 11, 1887 = Middleton #158
141   EH wise.8
142   One might explain away the contrast by noting that the first quote comes from a letter which, being addressed to a single person, is thus appropriate for confessions, while the second comes from a published work in which Nietzsche is deliberately trying to sound triumphant. But in light of the former the latter still comes off as false.

and his correspondence, but close enough. Around the edges of the ground floor are shops, including a dingy used bookstore that looks like it may well date from the late 1800's and, if so, surely entertained the Finos' shabbily-dressed boarder many, many times. I step in for a few moments to soak up the atmosphere.

We want to go upstairs to where Nietzsche's room would have been, but the staircases are roped off and a sign says *chiuso*. We could step over the insubstantial barriers easily and find our way up to the southwest corner of the top floor where Nietzsche's room was located. I consider this for a minute, but in the end decide to respect the signs, which might well be there because those on the upper floors are annoyed by tourist intrusions.

Was it unfaithful to Nietzsche to be so well-behaved? His writing and philosophy are transgressive, but accounts of him personally paint him as mild-mannered and polite. What if we had gone up? What would we have seen? Just a closed and locked door, I'm sure. On the other hand, what could it have hurt? At the worst, we'd have gotten yelled at and chased back downstairs.

But exit we do, via the other end of the building, onto Piazza Carignano, and we look back up to find his window. And what do you know? That side of the building is … covered in scaffolding! Yes! It's *chiuso per restauro*! Twenty-five years after being stymied over and over by *chiuso per restauro* on my earlier visit to Italy, with my parents and siblings, I return with my wife and children to track down traces of Nietzsche and in doing so, am stymied by … *chiuso per restauro*. Sigh.

We are about to turn away and head across the *piazza* when I notice a plaque on the corner of the building. Here it is, first in Italian, then translated (with some added clarifications), followed by some comments:

IN QUESTA CASA
FEDERICO NIETZSCHE
CONOBBE LA PIENEZZA DELLO SPIRITO
CHE TENTA L'IGNOTO
LA VOLONTA' DI DOMINIO
CHE SUSCITA L'EROE

QUI
AD ATTESTARE L'ALTO DESTINO
E IL GENIO
SCRISSE "ECCE HOMO"
LIBRO DELLA SUA VITA

A RICORDO
DELLE ORE CREATRICI
PRIMAVERA AUTUNNO 1888
NEL LO CENTENARIO DELLA NASCITA
LA CITTÁ DI TORINO
POSE
15 OTTOBRE 1944 A. XXII E.F.

In this house
Federico Nietzsche
Realized the fullness of the spirit
Which tests the unknown
The will to power
That rouses the hero

Who
In order to attest to his highest destiny
And to his genius
Wrote "Ecce Homo,"
The book of his life

To the memory
Of its creator [who lived here in]

Spring [and] Autumn 1888
[On the occasion of] the centenary of his birth
The city of Turin
Placed [this plaque]
15 October 1944
22nd year of the establishment of Fascism

First thing to point out about this plaque is that, although Nietzsche wrote several other books while in Turin, mentioning *Ecce Homo* alone is actually not inappropriate. *Ecce Homo* is indeed "the book of his life"—that is, his autobiography—and at the beginning of that book, Nietzsche notes that he is writing on his 44th birthday, October 15, 1888. Just as surely as one's birthday is an appropriate moment to begin one's autobiography, so too those who are placing a plaque in honor of the centenary of his birthday—October 15, 1944—do well to recall that particular work when they do so.

Second, note that at the time the plaque was being mounted the Fascists were still in charge of Turin. Turin, located in the northernmost part of Italy, was not liberated until late April, 1945, just a couple of weeks before the end of the war. The way the Fascists marked time itself as dating from the beginning of their rule might seem outrageously egotistical but in fact is a tradition on this peninsula: The Roman Empire counted years "AUC", i.e. *ab urbe condita*, i.e. from the founding of the city of Rome.

Finally, note the mention of the will to power. Most people who don't know much about Nietzsche know this phrase—it's the one his sister used as the title for the book she constructed out of some notebook fragments—and most of those people assume it refers to power in the sense of political or personal domination. Such people will find it unsurprising that the Fascists mention the will to power on this plaque. However, political power is not actually what Nietzsche means by the phrase and in fact, if you look again, it doesn't mean political power even in its use on this plaque. Rather, what Nietzsche means by 'will to power' is the will to have an effect on the world. Here's one of the more extended passages in which he explains what he means:

> Suppose ... we succeeded in explaining our entire instinctive life as the development and ramification of one basic form of the will—namely, of the will to power, as *my* proposition has it; suppose all organic functions could be traced back to this will to power and one could also find in it the solution of the problem of procreation and nourishment —it is *one* problem—then one would have gained the right to determine *all* efficient force univocally as—*will to power*. The world viewed from inside, the world defined and determined according to its 'intelligible character'—it would be 'will to power' and nothing else.[143]

Don't be distracted by the uncertain tone of "suppose" and "could" and "would"—Nietzsche's use of the 'will to power' concept throughout his later works makes clear he thinks this is in fact the best interpretation available for understanding human behavior. What he's pointing out, I believe, is that people do whatever they can to have an effect on the world. Thus toddlers scribble on the walls, children draw on paper, adults paint on canvas, those who can't paint write art criticism or say petulant things about art they can't understand, and so on. One might deliberately refrain from

---

143   BGE 36

painting to do something else at which one thinks one will be more effective, or simply to conserve one's energy for something else. One might even be mistaken about that and make poor choices, not understanding one's true powers, effects and opportunities. The point is that all of us seek to affect the world in whatever ways and to whatever extent we can. This is what Nietzsche calls our will to power.[144]

Nietzsche thinks this is applicable to the non-human world as well, and not just to animals but to plants—saplings compete for air and nutrients, pine trees try to keep the rest of the forest's vegetation down, etc. In this he is following Schopenhauer, who said that our inner access to ultimate reality in our own cases—i.e. our recognition from the "inside" that we have will—should be extended to the "inside" of all entities, and thus rocks, tables, chairs, *et cetera* have will too—they will themselves to remain in place, to support things placed on them, and so on. Nietzsche's addition to Schopenhauer is to say it's not simply will—Schopenhauer used the phrase "will to live," which Nietzsche says is silly, since these things are already alive—but will *to power*.

Political power is one form of power, of course. It might well be the way in which some people seek to exercise their will to power, and it might well be a very effective way to do so. However, a person might refrain from seeking political power from precisely the same instinct—one might recognize that this next election cannot be won and thus writing a book about one's ideas will have the most effect, or one might be too tired for another campaign. One can always be mistaken about the best way to exercise one's power.

The best illustration of the fact that Nietzsche's concept of the will to power does not necessarily involve overt political

144   In this passage "will to power"—in German *wille zur macht*—is used in apposition with "efficient force," the German for which is *kraft*, which could also be translated as "strength" or "energy."

domination is that the person who had the most will to power in history, by Nietzsche's lights, was Socrates, who never exercised any overt political power but was able to get succeeding generations, for 2400 years now, to think like him, i.e. to care about logical consistency.[145] Remember also the mention of the will to power in that paragraph about architecture I quoted above in connection with the Molé. The architect's will to power is to defy gravity, not conquer people. Nietzsche says in that paragraph that architects are *inspired* by powerful people, by which he might mean politically powerful—and this might explain why Nietzsche so often turns, for examples, to such people as Napoleon and the Borgias—but will to power is a much broader and, for that reason, a much more interesting concept.

Nietzsche's own exercise of the will to power is to get us to think a certain way, to try out certain thoughts. And this is in fact the sense of the phrase as it appears on the plaque. Perhaps the person who composed the plaque actually knew more about Nietzsche than the Fascists who hired him. The Fascists took Nietzsche to be their ideologue, but they did not in fact understand him, and thus they did not truly follow in his footsteps despite their claims.

The plaque is an unexpected find—it is not mentioned in the Krell book—and so compensates for the frustrating scaffolding and *chiuso per restauro*.

TIRED and hot, we turn around 180 degrees from the southwest corner of the Galleria Subalpina and see, in the southwest corner of the Piazza Carignano, a *gelato* shop—a most welcome sight.

---

145   T II.2 and 5

Nietzsche, by the way, loved chocolate and loved ice cream. I have always found this a wonderfully humanizing aspect of his biography. In *Twilight of the Idols*, written right here in Turin shortly after he arrived in the spring, in the course of explaining his view that we often confuse cause and effect, he says:

> I give an example. Everybody[146] knows the book of the famous Cornaro in which he recommends his slender diet as a recipe for a long and happy life—a virtuous one too. Few books have been read so much; even now thousands of copies are sold in England every year. I do not doubt that scarcely any book (except the Bible, as is meet) has done as much harm, has *shortened* as many lives, as this well-intentioned *curiosum*. The reason: the mistaking of the effect for the cause. The worthy Italian thought his diet was the *cause* of his long life, whereas the precondition for a long life, the extraordinary slowness of his metabolism, the consumption of so little, was the cause of his slender diet. He was not free to eat little *or* much; his frugality was not a matter of 'free will': he became sick when he ate more.... A long life, many descendants— this is not the wages of virtue; rather virtue itself is that slowing down of the metabolism which leads, among other things, also to a long life, many descendants—in short, to *Cornarism*.[147]

---

146   Everybody, that is, except most of my readers, but don't worry, I had to look it up too: Cornaro was a Renaissance-era Venetian nobleman who, facing serious illness at age 35, began to seriously restrict his calories, and then wound up living to almost 100.

147   Before the ellipsis is T VI.1, after is T VI.2.

This diet worked for Cornaro, according to Nietzsche, not because it *made* him healthy, but because he began already with a slender build that made the diet appropriate for him—thus he confused cause and effect. This led him, in turn, to think the same cause would have the same effect on everyone. This, says Nietzsche (elsewhere), is classic moralism—asserting that everyone should do what is appropriate for one person: "Some moralists want to vent their power and creative whims on humanity; some others … suggest with their morality: 'What deserves respect in me is that I can obey—and you *ought* not to be different from me.'"[148]

But Nietzsche *was* different from Cornaro, and he cannot resist here scoring points not only about mistaken causation, and about moralism, but about individualism as well. In the ellipsis above he writes:

> But whoever is no carp not only does well to eat properly, but needs to. A scholar in our time, with his rapid consumption of nervous energy, would simply destroy himself with Cornaro's diet. *Crede experto.*[149]

The last phrase is Latin for "believe the expert"—Nietzsche means he is an expert about himself, and others who might think to give him advice—such as Cornaro—should acknowledge that expertise. Apparently Nietzsche felt he, himself, needed to eat more than Cornaro recommended, and of course, with all that walking he did, he probably did need all those calories (the doctors' log at the sanatorium recorded that he had a voracious appetite). And this is sufficient justification, in his book (and mine), for his (and our) chocoholism.

148   BGE 187
149   T VI.2.

ON my way to exchange money at the Porta Nuova during that afternoon's "feet-up time," I see a commercial being filmed right around the corner from us, on Via Lagrange. I can't quite tell what it's for (isn't that true with so many commercials?), possibly for some sort of deodorant, because the filming consists of a troop of guys in sports uniforms running past a beautiful girl, who turns and waves. There are several different troops of men in several different types of sports uniforms, and they are each filmed in exactly the same way doing exactly the same thing. Maybe the film crew is seeing which group looks best? Or maybe there will be several iterations of this commercial?

I join a crowd on the opposite sidewalk watching the proceedings. As it happens I am standing next to the beautiful girl's handlers, a very homely and scruffy-looking pair of people who rush over to her between takes. They primp her hair and dry her brow while she stands still and benignly allows them to take care of her. Then as the camera rolls she greets the jogging athletes with a big wave and sweet smile as if she knows each and every one of them and is so very glad to see them. Then the camera stops and she resumes standing still and expressionless while her handlers primp her again.

This is an occasion to share one of my favorite passages in Nietzsche. It's an obscure one, usually cited, if at all, as an example of Nietzsche's misogyny. There's no question that Nietzsche is a misogynist of some sort. Given his ineffective mother, hellish sister and the fact that the only woman he ever loved ran off with his best friend, his attitude is not surprising. It is a bit surprising that he should see fit to express these prejudices in his writing, but even that might have more to do with his point that we all have prejudices of some kind or other. At any rate, that's how I read passages like this one:

> Whenever a cardinal problem is at stake, there speaks an unchangeable 'this is I'; about man and woman, for example, a thinker cannot relearn but only finish learning—only discover ultimately how this is 'settled in him.' At times we find certain solutions of problems that inspire strong faith in *us*; some call them henceforth *their* 'convictions.' Later—we see them only as steps to self-knowledge, sign-posts to the problem we *are*—rather, to the great stupidity we are, to our spiritual *fatum*, to what is 'unteachable' very deep down.
>
> After this abundant civility that I have just evidenced in relation to myself I shall perhaps be permitted more readily to state a few truths about 'woman as such'—assuming that it is now known from the outset how very much these are after all only—*my* truths.[150]

He then launches into a string of chauvinistic passages, which I will not dignify by repeating here. With such an introduction, though, you have to wonder whether he means them seriously or not, if they're only *his* truths. He does mean them, I think, but he recognizes that there's no reason for readers to agree, since they don't have the same prejudices—that's why he emphasizes that these are only *his* truths. So those comments are somewhat insulated from the

---

150   BGE 231

rest of his views. The reader can disregard them and still take seriously the rest of what he has to say (for example, the lovely statement about "steps to self-knowledge").

At any rate, I don't think that what's going on in this next passage can be dismissed as simple male chauvinism. See what you think:

> *Women and their action at a distance* – ...
> Here I stand in the flaming surf whose white tongues are licking at my feet; from all sides I hear howling, threats, screaming, roaring coming at me, while the old earth-shaker sings his aria in the lowest depths, ... while pounding such an earth-shaking beat that the hearts of even those weather-beaten rocky monsters are trembling in their bodies. Then, suddenly, as if born out of nothing, there appears before the gate of this hellish labyrinth, only a few fathoms away—a large sailboat, gliding along as silently as a ghost. Oh, what ghostly beauty! How magically it touches me! Has all the calm ... of the world embarked on it?... A spirit-like intermediate being: quietly observing, gliding, floating? As the boat that with its white sails moves like an immense butterfly over the dark sea. Yes! To move *over* existence! That's it! That would be something!
>
> ... All great noise leads us to move happiness into some quiet distance. When a man stands in the midst of his own noise, in the midst of his own surf of plans and projects, then he is apt also to see quiet, magical beings gliding past him and to long for their happiness and seclusion: *women*. He almost thinks that his better self dwells

there among the women, and that in these quiet regions even the loudest surf turns into deathly quiet, and life itself into a dream about life. Yet! Yet! Noble enthusiast, even on the most beautiful sailboat there is a lot of noise, and unfortunately much small and petty noise. The magic and the most powerful effect of women is, in philosophical language, action at a distance, *actio in distans*; but this requires first of all and above all— distance.[151]

What a great metaphor: Women of that time period, wearing long, full dresses that covered their legs and even their feet, must indeed have appeared to have been gliding effortlessly across the surface of the world like full-rigged sailboats with the wind at their backs. But Nietzsche's general idea here, that beauty haunts us with the prospect of a halcyon escape from our own troubled situation, is also brilliant and I believe, works equally well, regardless of one's object of desire. And in both cases, whether we see our escape from our own noise in the presence of a beautiful woman or a beautiful man, we are inevitably surprised to find, when we get close to him or her, ordinary human noise. Why, they're human just like us! And to be with them, then, would be no escape. The passage, on my reading, doesn't attack women but rather exhorts us to face up to our own problems, without illusions.

Puncturing illusions is much of what Nietzsche's entire philosophy is all about. And I reflect too, as I walk on, that his point about the illusion of escape really applies to this whole commercial-filming scene, not just to that artificially maintained beautiful woman but to the whole world of

151   GS 60

television advertising, a world where our noise, our pain, our striving melt away in a veneer of happy perfection.

Sure enough, after changing money at the train station, I return to find all of them—the beautiful woman, her handlers, the sports guys, the camera crew—vanished like some charmed illusion.

Vanished just like Lou Salomé from Nietzsche's life.

SHE was beautiful and brilliant, destined to become an accomplished author in her own right, including a book on Nietzsche's philosophy that is actually pretty good (advantaged, of course, by a degree of access to him that no one else ever had). She went on afterwards to be an intellectual and romantic companion to many of the leading male intellectual lights of the day, including the poet Rilke and, late in her life, Freud. She was only twenty when she met Nietzsche but already sophisticated and well-read, a Russian who had already traveled most of Europe and spoke several of its languages.

They met in April 1882, in Rome.[152] Nietzsche's friend Paul Rée, a thinker and writer who had been an important influence in Nietzsche's break with Wagner and in his writings in the late 1870's, told Nietzsche he had someone he wanted him to meet. Nietzsche must have thought Rée was meaning to fix him up romantically, because when he met Lou[153]—

---

152   For the whole Lou Salomé story, see the Hayman biography, Chapter 9.

153   I have always thought of her as Lou, and she has generally been referred to by her first name by past scholars and biographers of Nietzsche, so I will continue to do that here, although I admit that I don't do that with Nietzsche or Rée. The copy editor for my first book called me on the carpet about this and correctly pointed out that there's an aspect of male chauvinism in referring to a woman by her first name at the same time as referring to a man by his last name, so in that book I changed all the references from "Lou" to "Salomé." Here, though, I'm going to revert to using "Lou"—it just seems appropriately intimate for the only

in St. Peter's basilica in the Vatican, a remarkably dramatic setting, which surely contributed to his being swept up emotionally—he wondered out loud what star had brought them together. I picture her being flattered but also slightly embarrassed. I picture Rée starting to think this whole idea had been a mistake right off the bat.

Lou admired Nietzsche's genius and Nietzsche, for his part, wrote excitedly in his letters about possibly having found a disciple. The three friends—who referred to themselves as "the trinity"—spent several months in and out of each other's company that spring and summer, in various combinations of twos and threes, in various locations in Italy, Switzerland and Germany. Nietzsche's one-on-one time with Lou came in August, in the little town of Tautenberg, a Black Forest resort in southern Germany.

They took their meals and long walks together, sitting from time to time on benches that the town had put up especially for the Professor's visit. (This means, I think, that it was a pretty small town and also that Nietzsche had a bit more of a reputation back then than the traditional story of his life admits.) They stayed in separate lodgings, of course, as to do otherwise would have been inappropriate in that Victorian era. I wish that had been all the Victorianism there was, but unfortunately it was also considered necessary that Nietzsche's sister Elizabeth accompany them as chaperone. Sure enough, Lou and Elizabeth, who shared the train ride to Tautenberg, quarreled spitefully from the very beginning. Elizabeth was surely overprotective of her brother's "virtue," which was entirely unthreatened anyway, and Lou, brilliant, sophisticated and independent-minded as she was, was surely insulted by Elizabeth's frumpy condescension.

---

love of his life. Perhaps another reason I do so is that, like so many other male scholars of Nietzsche, I'm *rooting* for him, utterly and completely hopeless though his pursuit of her was.

So in a way it was idyllic for Nietzsche, probably the best fortnight in his life, a time filled with long walks and great conversation with a fascinating woman. But it must have been a nightmare also, to be in the company of his dream girl with an unpleasant, unwanted third wheel along, who just happened to be his sister. Lou could only take it for so long and left in a huff after two weeks. The "trinity" were together again in Leipzig in October, but Lou and Rée left there for Paris without Nietzsche and he never saw either of them again.

Was there ever a kiss? Years later, Lou couldn't remember for certain either way.   Did he ever propose to her? Lou claims he did so twice, but we can't be sure of that either, since she is writing many years after the fact and, according to many scholars, toying with us by playing up her role in his life. The letters we have contain some oblique references to conversations unrecorded and perhaps left dangling.

One thing I am sure of is that it was hopeless from the beginning. Rée had met her first, was closer to Lou in age than Nietzsche, and was much more socially well-adjusted, more a man of the world and even, in my admittedly subjective opinion, much more handsome. He and Lou addressed each other as *du*, the German second person singular that connotes equality and intimacy (similar to the French *tu*), while Nietzsche and Lou remained, at least in their letters, at the more formal level of *sie*. Nietzsche, meanwhile, was not only older but clearly saw her as a potential disciple, which I'm sure she hated.[154] Here's the *coup de grace*: We know a lot about Nietzsche's conversations with Lou only because of a document she wrote at the time for Rée himself, which she titled "Tautenberg Diary for Paul Rée;" she wrote no parallel "Diary for Friedrich Nietzsche" when she was with Rée.

---

154   Letter to Lou Salomé, June 26, 1882, in Krell & Bates 131

He was crushed, of course. At first, he took it out on his sister—which Elizabeth richly deserved even though I don't think the outcome would have been any different if she had not been there—writing furious letters and then not speaking to her for more than a year. He was depressed for a very long time, coming out of it only for a manic two-week period during which he wrote all of Book I of *Thus Spoke Zarathustra*, then being depressed again, then coming out of it for another manic two-week period during which he wrote all of Book II, then being depressed again, then discovering Nice and climbing the hill at Èzé and writing Book III during another manic two-week period. Then he was himself again and resumed correspondence with his sister.

Both Lou and Rée are mentioned in *Ecce Homo* and, remarkably, neither reference is at all vindictive. You'll recall from the three-day migraine passage in that same book that Nietzsche teaches us to live well not merely in spite of, but *because of* the blows we suffer. And at this late date, six years after the disaster and roughly six weeks before his breakdown, Nietzsche graciously acknowledges that Rée had been an important influence on his intellectual development[155], and that Lou had written the poem which constitutes the text of *Das Hymnus ad Leben*, "The Hymn to Life," their collaboration for which Nietzsche had composed the music and which was published in 1886.[156]

And now perhaps you are wondering what I always wonder when I consider this story: *What if she had said 'yes'?* We don't know if he actually did propose, of course, and I don't think he ever had much of a real shot with her, but suppose he had and suppose she had accepted—what would have become of his philosophy? Would he still have been such

---

155   EH books.HAH.6
156   EH books.Z.1

a passionate advocate of individualism? More precisely, what would his thoughts about individualism have become if he had been forced to maintain his individuality in the context of an extended romantic relationship? Or even—and here we're really getting into science fiction in terms of the two people involved[157]—in the context of a family with children?

This is where Nietzsche is of no help to us at all. He does have occasional comments on the topic of marriage and children, such as this speech from *Thus Spoke Zarathustra*:

> You are young and wish for a child and marriage. But I ask you: Are you a man entitled to wish for a child? Are you the victorious one, the self-conqueror, the commander of your senses, the master of your virtues?
>
> Let your victory and your freedom long for a child. You shall build living monuments to your victory and your liberation. You shall build over and beyond yourself, but first you must be built yourself, perpendicular in body and soul. You shall not only reproduce yourself, but produce something higher. May the garden of marriage help you in that!
>
> You shall create a higher body, a first movement, a self-propelled wheel—you shall create a creator.
>
> Marriage: thus I name the will of two to

---

157   Lou eventually married a man named Friedrich Andreas (so she is often referred to in the literature as Lou Andreas-Salomé) a few years later, making it clear to him when he proposed that she had no intention of sleeping with him and so the marriage would be a social arrangement only. She did, however, sleep with several other members of the male intellectual elite who were her companions. But she never had any children. To pursue her story would take me too far from mine, but I encourage you to look her up—she was a strong, free, proudly intellectual woman in a time period when this combination was widely frowned upon. And to Nietzsche's credit, he loved her for it.

create the one that is more than those who
created it. Reverence for each other, as for
those willing with such a will, is what I name
marriage.[158]

The fact that he wrote this just months after the disaster
with Lou is a remarkable expression of faith in marriage as
an ideal. And so I wish Nietzsche had had to confront the
issues that inevitably arise in an actual marriage, because
I'm sure, with his tremendous intelligence and psychological
sensitivity, he would have had wonderfully insightful things
to say about them. As it is, despite that lovely passage from
Zarathustra, he's not much help in this regard.

And so as we leave Turin I'm feeling estranged from him
again, as I did the day we arrived. I find this odd, since I
expected to love Turin as he did. But for some reason our
differences—on marriage, religion, family, elitism, etc.—
came out here in ways they didn't in Nice. He left here
without his mind, and I feel like I'm leaving here without
him too, in a sense.

MP3s & Veltliner

THERE'S A GREAT scene in the movie *Patton* in which the title character is watching proudly as his troops march dutifully through the snow in December, 1944, on a forced march to relieve the siege at Bastogne, and he says to his aide-de-camp, "This is where it pays off: the training, the discipline."

We're not marching in the snow or anything. Still, that's how I feel now at 0500 hours as everyone quietly goes about the necessary dressing and washing and final packing and gets out the door, and again at 0530 as the Professional Travelers troop silently towards Stazione di Porta Nuova. There's no complaining, no squabbling, no friction—just calm cooperation and getting the job done. It feels like a successful project Vicky and I have completed together, although I'm not sure exactly what we did right with these children to make this sort of early departure go so smoothly—establish discipline early maybe, or make clear we wouldn't ask them to do anything we wouldn't do ourselves, or maybe not push against the current when we don't have to. Maybe it's just pure luck. They have turned out well, as Nietzsche would say, competent and cooperative and creative and strong—that which did not kill them made them stronger.

It's one of his most famous sayings and also one of the most misunderstood. People often quote it as if it's some sort of inviolable natural law: that which does not kill you makes you stronger. In that form, though, it's patently false, since people sometimes come out of accidents as paraplegics, un-killed but also definitely not stronger. What Nietzsche actually wrote, though, right here in Turin in the spring of 1888, was a brief aphorism—*"Out of life's school of war: What does not destroy me, makes me stronger."*[159] It's not a natural law, but rather a hard-earned personal insight. Later that year, back in town after his summer in Sils, he expanded on the idea in his autobiography:

> What is it, fundamentally, that allows us to recognize *who has turned out well?* ... He has a taste only for what is good for him; his pleasure, his delight cease where the measure of what is good for him is transgressed. He guesses what remedies avail against what is harmful; he exploits bad accidents to his advantage; what does not kill him makes him stronger.[160]

The description goes on, but you get the point: Nietzsche is describing someone *who has already* turned out well—*looking back*, it can be seen that whatever did not kill him made him stronger. But it isn't an automatic rule. It's a good ideal to have, of course, and if you're ever in bad circumstances it's a good mantra to hold in mind to rally yourself. Like Nietzsche with his migraines, you have to figure out for yourself how to grow from your injuries and how to utilize your setbacks in order to move forward. But it doesn't just happen on its own.

---

159   T I.8
160   EH wise.2

THE 0600 train from Turin to Milan is a businesspersons' express. Our tourist garb and baggage stand out. We go foraging for food at the *stazione Milano* and though we're ready to settle for anything edible, we find not only some excellent pastries but also *gianduiotto*—a hazelnut-flavored chocolate spread invented in Turin and soon to be marketed in North America as Nutella—sold in a packet with a handful of skinny breadsticks, called *grissini*, to dip in it. Now *this* is a proper breakfast-on-the-go. Well-furnished with our deluxe victuals, we get on the train to Tirano. After some more time with the flat fields and villages of northern Italy, the geography starts to change.

The train runs along the eastern shore of Lake Como. We pass through a series of picturesque villages: Lierna, Fiumelatte, Varenna, Bellano. Even the train stations here have ornate decorative gewgaw around their slate roofs. The opposite shore is mostly without buildings, just forested mountainsides plunging straight into the lake. The escarpment levels out at the end of the peninsula that divides Lake Como into a wishbone shape, and there's Bellagio, stunningly perched on the land's very tip. The water is deep blue, the vistas breathtaking.

I notice that my children all have their MP3's on. Nietzsche would have *loved* having an MP3 player, absolutely loved it. After all, this is the guy who wrote, "Without music, life would be an error."[161] An MP3 player would have allowed him to use music to charm his soul continuously. Maybe he would have even gotten sick less often. But it would have increased his isolation too. Whenever he heard music he was in the presence of other people, even if it was hearing strains wafted in from a café around the corner, or from down in the atrium of the Galleria Subalpina up to his room on the

---

161   T I.33

fourth floor.[162] In our time we listen to music primarily in recorded, disembodied form. It's wonderful to have it so often and so available, of course, but possibly it's become a cheaper, shallower experience. And maybe it's not so good for music to be ubiquitous.

NEAR the lake's northern end, the train turns eastward up a little valley with almost sheer sides. It's not much wider than the railroad right-of-way, but what little flat space there is teems with grape vines, and in fact even the sheer sides are planted too. It's an ingenious use of space: The sides of the valley are too steep for terrace farming, but since grape vines are pinned to wooden frames anyway, they'll grow just fine provided the frames are secured to the hillsides. It's utterly charming, this narrow gorge green with grape leaves and barely enough room for a train to squeeze through.

At the top of the valley is Tirano, the last town in Italy before you cross into Switzerland. We leave the train and find a place to eat and come happily across Ristorante Vittoria. I hatched a plan some years ago to try to sample every single restaurant in the world that's named after my wife, and we did indeed eat at one such in Turin, so right now my plan is proceeding apace. But here's the coolest thing about the restaurant: A paragraph on the menu (available in English) explains that the valley we've just ridden through is called Valtellina, and it offers us wine from the grapes grown there. And this little menu note doesn't sound like much to my family, but for me it is an absolutely mind-blowing revelation. For suddenly a line in one of Nietzsche's last letters, written just after his breakdown but before he lost all his functioning,

---

162   Letter to Peter Gast, December 16, 1888 = Middleton #191.

makes sense.

On the cusp of his madness, Nietzsche invited Burckhardt to join him in Turin and, trying to convey the civilized pleasures that could be had there, says, "A glass of Veltliner could be obtained."[163] The name of that drink always reminds me of an ocean liner, or maybe the old Amtrak Metroliner I would sometimes ride during my nomadic student days. But I never really knew what it was. Now however, after twenty-nine years of puzzling over this line, sitting in the Ristorante Vittoria in Tirano, Italy, I suddenly get it: Veltliner is the German way to say Valtellina, and of course a wine grown here could be expected to be available in Turin.[164] The valley we've just ridden through on the train is the place where that wine was grown and bottled. By the time Burckhardt actually arrived in Turin, Nietzsche had dropped completely into his madness and so I'm sure that glass of Veltliner was never drunk. But now that obscure reference in that last, crazy letter makes some sense to me.

The next night, at our hotel in Sils-Maria, I will ask for a glass of Veltliner and succeed in obtaining one. I will toast my family, and toast Nietzsche. He didn't get to have that drink with Burckhardt, but he did with me.

It was worth coming all this way.

---

163   This is the letter that's dated January 6 but was postmarked January 5, 1889, found in the *Portable Nietzsche* 686.
164   During revision of this manuscript, I have learned that Veltliner is widely produced in central Europe, so I can't be sure the glasses of it I drank in Sils-Maria actually came from the Valtellina (they never showed me the bottles). But I remain convinced that the name of the wine did.

Ascent to Sils-Maria

ONE CAN GET from Milan to Sils-Maria more directly by taking the train to Chiavenna and then the bus through the Engadin valley. Instead, we have traveled by way of Tirano deliberately to board the legendary Bernina Express. Sam came across it while doing his Europe research and loaded his votes on it and we were all happy to go along with his idea. We hoped it would change the train ride from being just a means to get somewhere into being part of the journey. But it turns out to be even more than we imagined.

We already have our tickets, purchased online long ago, but we must still present our passports in the little building that doubles as ticket booth and passport control. The contrast between the ordinary landscape we're in now and the extraordinary one we're about to go through makes me think later of that little shack as a secret portal to a hidden, dreamlike world.

The train is painted a brilliant red. The first two cars are normal motorized electric train cars, but the rest, including ours, are specially built panorama cars, short and boxy, with very comfortable seats and with windows that reach from near the floor till well into the ceiling, curving at the upper corners to allow for an undistorted view. We take over the rear section of one of these panorama cars and the train slides gently into motion.

At first the view is just more of the village of Tirano. The

Swiss train leaves on tracks parallel to the ones the Italian train arrived on, but then turns uphill. We ride closely by houses and right through fields, and it's charming to be part of the landscape. Unlike so many trains, especially those I'm used to riding in the northeastern US, which have routes through industrialized districts which by now are often bombed-out versions of their former selves, this one takes us right along active streets and through lived-in front yards, as if we're on some sort of model train display board. We work our way through the upper part of Tirano, passing people pinning up laundry, cars heading to the store, and houses covered by slate-shingled roofs with rows of little metal posts at the edges to break up the snow so it will slide off.

After a few minutes in town we start climbing along a gorge with a rushing river, trading places with a road trying to share the same narrow space. Later work with a map tells me this is the point at which we cross into Switzerland, although the actual border is unmarked as far as I can tell. And now the analogy to a model train set gets even closer: The train twists and turns, switchbacking from side to side, using the sides of the little valley to gain elevation. At one point it makes a remarkable full three hundred and sixty degree roundabout— circling around itself in order to access a bridge built above itself—so it can continue in the same direction on a viaduct raised above its previous level. Even on a sheet of plywood in the basement this would be a *tour de force*. It's hard for us to see for ourselves just yet why the train needs this much elevation, but it's easy to imagine that it surely will. The engineers must have calculated the elevation they'd need miles away, further up the pass, so they started raising the tracks way back here. Now we're looking down at the picturesque villages below and behind us as we head for the top of the pass.

At a station named Miralago—Lakeview—we look out

over Lago di Poschiavo and see, off in the distance, under a cloudy sky and above the lake's serene, steel gray surface, the southern flank of the Alps. And now, having risen above the everyday, ordinary life of the town, we're ready to take the philosopher's vantage point. Nietzsche, gushing about how Bizet's music makes him feel like more of a philosopher, describes that vantage point as follows:

> The gray sky of abstraction rent as if by lightning; the light strong enough for the filigree of things; the great problems near enough to grasp; the world surveyed as from a mountain—I have just described the pathos of philosophy.[165]

The philosopher's vantage point is still a perspective, not a God's-eye view—it's still earthbound and human. But it's a different perspective than the everyday, concerned not with getting things done but with their value and significance. Positioned high enough to see above and beyond the small things, we are ready to consider life as a whole and ponder its possible meanings.

WE head straight for those mountains that were formerly in the distance and are soon among them, weaving through passes that were not apparent from far away. It's an engineering marvel, this train line, hacked out of the rock, twisting and turning between cliffs and tarns. Several times the train switches back and forth via hairpin turns to go up a mountainside; at other points there's no other way to continue upward except by tunnels. Whatever the engineers needed to do, they did, and now we ascend effortlessly into the Alps.

There are, to be sure, signs of pre-railroad civilization up here too. The Romans came through centuries ago (which is why in Sils we'll be speaking a language called Romansh), and the Bernina pass has remained settled through at least twenty centuries. The ancient road, now nicely paved, shares space with the railroad right-of-way. Along the combined road/rail passage, tiny towns cling to a mountainside or hunker down in a little gorge. Here and there a herd of cows or sheep sip from a mountain stream.

As we go higher, though, civilization falls away, and the scenery becomes simply jaw-dropping. Each turn brings another vista—towering piles of rock with skullcaps of snow, separated by plunging valleys of greensward. Sometimes the pass we're traveling through deepens into a tarn, the green water made milky by glacial run-off. Sometimes in the distance we can see a waterfall, or even a snowfield. At one point we come close enough to see snow right by the tracks, stretching out away from us like a white river. And always there are the mountains, huge and inevitable, standing out from the earth in their bulk.

THERE'S something about the sight of mountains in the distance that raises one's soul. In part it's simply because responding to a mountain's verticality requires raising one's head. But it's also because responding to a mountain's elevation and severity requires activating one's energy and attention—one feels challenged by mountains. And yet at the same time their unmovable immensity provides calm and reassurance. In short, one must become a mountain oneself to look at them properly. Opening our eyes to high mountains, we prepare to live as our highest selves.

I stand motionless at the back of the rail car, right up against the panoramic window, staring at rows of distant peaks as we rumble along the roof of the earth. I imagine stretching my arms out to those mountains and around them, giving an impossible hug to our massive planet, object of Zarathustra's love:

> Remain faithful to the earth, my brothers, with the power of your virtue. Let your gift-giving love and your knowledge serve the meaning of the earth…. Alas, there has always been so much virtue that has flown away. Lead back to the earth the virtue that flew away, as I do—back to the body, back to life, that it may give the earth a meaning, a human meaning.[166]

Some people, at this elevation, would think of themselves as closer to heaven, but for Nietzsche, regarding the earth from a height leads only to fiercer love for it, and to a determination not to live as an immaterial soul nor merely await an unworldly afterlife. This earth, in all its physical beauty, calls out for the meaning we would give it.

A line of Nietzsche's which is oft-quoted these days is this:

> [W]hen you look long into an abyss, the abyss also looks long into you.[167]

But in fact he looked up much more often than he looked

---

166   Z I.22.2
167   BGE 146

down, and he took continual inspiration from mountains. Nietzsche is not a valley philosopher, he's a mountain philosopher, and I feel like I'm regaining my touch with his spirit just by looking long at these mountains.

AT some point, the train crests the Bernina Pass. There's no marker; one just gradually gets the sense that the climb is over and the train is now descending gently. There are indicators, of course—the streams and freshets now rush in the same direction as the train instead of back behind us. The scenery changes too: Instead of rough, rocky scree and glaciers, there is now wild vegetation. Later, there is cultivated vegetation and still later, more settlement.

The train tracks wind back and forth across the paved road and the switchbacks are so close together that one end of the train stops traffic at a crossing down here while the other end is still stopping traffic at another crossing back there. After the bare rock atop the mountains there are now forests, and we're close enough to the hiking paths that we can see and, if the train stops close enough, even read the directional signs by the paths. Such proximity between a working train line and hiking paths wouldn't happen back in America. Hiking in Switzerland is more civilized, more domesticated than in America, despite the dramatic severity of the Alps. It actually appeals to me more—I don't believe that natural beauty exists only when untouched by humans. Humans can improve things, make them more beautiful, by working with nature. Instead of seeing an opposition between appreciating beauty and creating it, we should think of our creative activity as helping beauty along, like gardeners training morning glories to grow up a trellis, or engineers carving a railway grade along a hillside, or writers recognizing as stories the lives they've actually lived.

After our spectacular trip from Tirano up through the Bernina Pass and across the top of the world and down into Switzerland—a train ride out of a child's fantasy, gliding through a dreamscape, a world of greenery and picturesque villages, tracks laid as for a model train, pristine ponds, grade-crossings over hiking paths, churches in the middle of hillsides reached only on foot, the train tracks interweaving with the road—after gazing at glaciers and ripple-less lakes, after reaching out and touching the clouds at the tips of the mountains on the roof of the world, we touch down again in St. Moritz (as if the train had been an airplane and now we were landing on the ground again) and find the bus that will take us to Sils-Maria.

Living Dangerously

IN AMERICA, when we speak of a two-street town we mean two streets that intersect at right angles, one running east-west and the other north-south, forming a cross and dividing the town into quadrants. It's a classic American type.

Sils, however, is a two-street town of a very different type: There are a total of two streets in the entire town. "First-class as landscape," Nietzsche said of it,[168] and here's its layout: The town sits in the middle of a glacial gorge running northeast to southwest that's only about a thousand meters wide measured northwest to southeast. "Glacial gorge" means it is utterly flat in the middle, with steep, rocky, forested sides. To the southwest is Lake Sils, to the northeast Lake Silvaplana. Along the northwest edge, on the far side of the lakes and right up against the mountain known as Piz Polaschin (Piz is the Romansh word for peak), runs the main road between St. Moritz (at the Swiss end) and Chiavenna (at the Italian end). Intersecting with the main road at two points about a kilometer apart are the two streets, which then run for about a kilometer each themselves until they intersect at the Sils town square. The two streets plus the main road thus form not a cross but an equilateral triangle in between the two lakes. Along the two streets are a mix of hotels, residences, offices and businesses, grouped into two parts: a larger one, where our hotel and the Nietzsche-*Haus* are located, called Sils-Maria, and a smaller one, closer to the main road, called

Sils-Baselgia. In the center of the triangle lies a vast open field packed with blooming wildflowers.

We have arrived in Sils at just the right time. The whole point of Nietzsche's three-residence scheme—Nice in winter, Sils in summer, Turin in the shoulder seasons—was to be in the right place at the right time of year. Our following in his footsteps has mostly so far missed the point. We don't have a whole year to do this, just two weeks, and unlike Nietzsche we have school year obligations. The time we have available to make this trip is late June and early July, no other options. When we were in Nice it was too hot, and when we were in Turin it was still too hot. Sils however, we have done just right—we have arrived in early summer, when the Alpine wildflowers bloom.

Picture an entire meadow filled with at least seventeen different varieties of wildflowers—some familiar from America, others local to the Alps, a happy cacophony of light blue and dark blue and white and lavender and orange and pink and yellow—the beautiful outcome of the deadly serious evolutionary struggle to get the bees' attention. No wonder Nietzsche came back at this time every year. This landscape, he wrote, "is intimate and familiar to me, related to me by blood, and by more than blood."[169]

WE step off the bus from St. Moritz at a little *platz* between two hotels and walk back maybe fifty meters to the Hotel Seraina.[170] Now it's Vicky's turn to take the language lead. I have to admit her rusty German does much better than my Berlitz-crammed Italian, as she manages to get us registered

169   WS 338, translated and quoted by Krell & Bates 150.
170   The name is a cognate of our word "serene," reflecting the Latinate side of Romansh.

without incident and without opera.

Most of the hotel's rooms are numbered, but the suites are named after Alpine flowers. Ours is the Enzian suite, which is an especially pretty little blue one, so we are pleased to call it home. We climb the stairs and unlock the door and enter. There's a little hallway that leads from the door and then around the corner, and then we step into the main part of the suite and our jaws drop.

There in front of us is a two-story window, and on the other side of the glass is Piz Polaschin, which somehow seems bigger and closer when framed this way, filling the window all by itself. It honestly looks for a minute as if that side of the suite actually consists of a two-story wall composed of an Alpine mountain draped in meadows of light green grass and copses of dark green pine, leading up to harsh, jagged, gray peaks.

After the initial visual shock, we can see that there's some distance between our window and the mountain. This distance contains a charming chalet with a slate roof just across the street, and on the far side of the chalet, a burbling brook running parallel to the street through a stone channel provided for it. Just beyond the brook there's that incredible field packed full of wildflowers, stretching perfectly flat all the way to the main road on the far side of the glacial valley. It's an amazing view and it's a sight we'll spend most of our time in the suite staring at.

THE Nietzsche-*Haus* is barely two hundred meters from our hotel. It looks just like it does in the photos I've seen—a square, two-story building under a steep, Alpine-style roof. The only thing the photos failed to show is that the house is set back from the street, allowing for a little walkway and a slightly dramatic approach—at least for one who has thought about coming here for so many years.

By the time we get there it's closed for the day, though, so all I can do is explore the exterior. I first head around to the right side of the house, knowing that that's the side with Nietzsche's window. The rear of the house is flush against the hill, so you can't easily walk around it—something else that's not apparent from the photos I've studied. So I circle back to check out the other side and there I find a surprise—a bin of books. A sign in German says (as far as I can make out) that this is a book exchange and that anyone can take and/or leave books to borrow, only the borrowers should please return the books without too much delay.

Something about this touches my fancy. Maybe it's the idea that Nietzsche, who lived such an isolated life, with so few people to discuss his ideas with, should now be the site for other intellectuals to share their books with each other. To be sure, he wasn't as isolated here in Sils-Maria as elsewhere. We know that there were other regular sojourners at Herr Gian Durisch's house—Nietzsche records once his annoyance at having to put down his pen to bid farewell to one of them leaving at the end of the season—and other seasonal visitors to the town with whom Nietzsche struck up friendships. Still, I think he'd be tickled to know that his house now hosts a book exchange.

NEXT morning, we return to the Nietzsche-*Haus*, walk around the building to the right, and find the path that begins below Nietzsche's window. I knew about it because there is a picture of it in the Krell and Bates book, taken from inside

Nietzsche's room. As soon as I saw that photo I wanted to hike that path, for the only way to describe that path in that photo is to say that it *beckons*. I imagine Nietzsche sitting at his writing table, scribbling a few words, looking up, looking longingly out the window and saying to himself: To hell with philosophy; I'm gonna go hike that path (or words to that effect in German). And now, here we are, standing right below that window, ready to go.

We head up the path, once again in Nietzsche's literal footsteps. Coming to the end of the first ascent through the woods behind the Nietzsche-*Haus*, our twelve eyes see the very same Alpine meadow that his two eyes saw one hundred and twenty-five years ago, just as gloriously full of wildflowers as I'm sure it was in the 1880's. It's a meadow of several acres, surrounded by trees, surrounded by mountains. All around us are white yarrow and orange hawkweed and pink geranium and lavender thalictrum and blue enzian and that dark-blue cupped one we don't know the name of and, in general, Alpine bliss.

The path climbs further, reenters the woods and turns back to the east. Around a bend there is a troop of cows, scattered through the trees, looking for bits of grass, their bells peacefully tinkling. Their ancestors surely told them stories about that very odd man Herr Doctor Professor Nietzsche, who walked by unfailingly at this time of year.[171] These cows, by the way, have arrived here the same way we did, by train. Yes, Swiss cows get summer vacations—having endured the Swiss winter in their barns eating hay, they get transported by special trains up to these Alpine meadows for the summer,

---

171   Students of German philosophy will recognize the allusion to Kant, whose afternoon walks were so regular, it was said, that the housewives of Königsberg set their clocks by his passing. I'm sure Nietzsche would have been perfectly happy if the only time keeping apparatuses which could be set according to his movements were calendars.

to feast on green grass and delectable flowers and to shed their stress so that their milk stays sweet. It's a better summer vacation than most humans get, I reckon.

Then more woods and more wildflowers: yellow trollius and Carpathian bluebells. The only buildings are isolated farmhouses and barns.

Near one of these barns, at a spot the map identifies as Alp Prasüra (elevation 1950 meters), the path becomes confusing. I'm trying to follow a description from literature we got at the hotel written by someone who gives guided walks which he claims are Nietzsche's own routes. I'm a little suspicious of these routes—some of them go quite high up the mountainside and I don't think Nietzsche went that high, since his poor eyesight would have made negotiating steep paths difficult. In a letter to his mother he says that paths "have to be specially arranged for me, half-blind as I am."[172] My bet is that he stayed mostly at these lower levels, never too far from the level floor of the glacial gorge. His most common walks, as far as I can tell, went around the two lakes or, at most, went up only a little ways into the Fex Valley.

At any rate, we are now trying to follow one of the routes in the pamphlet, but the description of the path doesn't quite match what we're seeing. So we hem and haw for a while and try a couple of different options, taking a few steps each way, to see what the paths look like a little further on. Another party of hikers comes along and points us to the path they think we must be looking for, so we head along it. And for a while it's fine, running transverse along the slope of the hill, the path still lined with wildflowers. From time to time, along the uphill side of the path, beautiful little waterfalls appear, formed from rivulets heading down the mountainside from further up with *alpenmohn* and that midnight-dark-blue

172   See Krell and Bates 122

flower we don't know the name of growing alongside. After a few minutes we walk under a cable car line which, although we don't know it yet, we will be riding tomorrow.

The path is so broad and lovely that we are puzzled by signs we begin to see that say "*Holzschlag*," with a big exclamation point in a triangle. We don't understand this at all. We learned last night at dinner that *schlag* is the German word for whipped cream—the kids thought it was hilarious—and at the sight of this sign Eli says, "Give me the cream-puff but *holz* the *schlag*," But there doesn't seem to be any whipped cream at all on this mountain path, nor any prospect for any until we return to the valley floor and find our restaurant for lunch. So what are they talking about?

Further on, the path is still broad and lovely, but there are other signs in other languages and eventually we find one that says, "*Coupe de bois*," and I recall from my trip to Paris years ago the big park called the Bois de Boulogne, so I know that that means 'wood' and *coupe*, of course, means a blow or a hit. But it isn't till we've proceeded much further on that we begin seeing downed trees. The path becomes choppy with twigs and fallen boughs, the detritus of logging—what we call in Maine "slash"—and we realize that we've stumbled onto a place where the forest is being actively logged. The signs with big exclamation points in triangles were meant to tell us not to come this way.

By now, though, we're well along the path we began at Alp Prasüra and the prospect of turning back is quite discouraging. We were hoping to walk eastward along the slope of the mountain far enough that when we descended we would be right by the famous pyramid-shaped boulder at which Nietzsche thought of the eternal recurrence and at which we are hoping to find the plaque with a quote from *Zarathustra* commemorating the event. We did not intend to walk through an active logging zone, past signs warning us not to.

Vicky and I consider the options and decide to press on. The three younger children are horrified by our recklessness, but Sam is bemused. He promises to get me a t-shirt when we return that says WWND. And what *would* Nietzsche do? The actual Nietzsche, as I've said, would not have been able to negotiate a path so strewn with obstacles. But Sam's right: The spiritual Nietzsche, the one who exhorted his readers to live dangerously, would have continued, knowing that this was *his* chosen path, the one conducive to *his* situation and goals, and would actually have relished the *frisson* of possible danger.

And so do we, as we press on with difficulty through slash that eventually becomes so thick we are walking as much as a meter above the trail rather than on it, stumbling through the stuff and occasionally losing our footing, listening carefully for the sound of chainsaws. In the end, however, we find no loggers at work, and so we have the ideal combination: the thrill of living dangerously without any actual danger.

AFTER brushing the leaves and wood chips from our clothes, and having found the broad, easy path that runs around Lake Silvaplana, we are once again, truly and undeniably, in Nietzsche's actual footsteps. This is a path I'm quite sure he walked frequently, heading towards the boulder he made famous. Despite the lengthy amount of time we've spent in the *holzschlag*, we haven't actually made much eastward progress, so we still have a fair ways to go along the lake path. We see other walkers and, now that the ground is level, several bikers going in both directions. The atmosphere is something like that of a large urban park: Bois de Boulogne, Kensington Gardens, Central Park. Plenty of time to imagine Nietzsche and his walking stick on such a day, admiring the blue, rippled water and breathing deep the fresh smell of the pines.

We round a corner and there's the boulder. Yes, it's just like in the photos I've seen, but there is still something special about seeing it in person and being able to touch it.[173] It's as tall as I am and really is shaped like a pyramid. I recognize it immediately as a glacial erratic. The word comes from the Latin word for wandering—these are boulders that have been carried by glaciers and then left behind as the glaciers melted. They are quite common in Maine. I've seen erratics of all sizes and shapes in all sorts of places, but never one quite like this before. Its striking pyramidal shape and position right next to the lake makes me wonder if this boulder's geological history might be different from that of the usual glacial erratics.

And suddenly I think I understand why Nietzsche had the thought of eternal recurrence just here. You stand by this remarkable, uniquely shaped boulder and reflect on how long it has been sitting there in that shape, and you look across this pristine lake at the incredible, almost-vertical mountainsides across the valley, and you consider how the Alps, though they are relatively young mountains, are nevertheless incredibly old and have been in this position so very, very long—long before there were roads in this valley, long before the Cohens arrived, long before Nietzsche arrived, long before Swiss cantons were formed, long before any German-speakers arrived, long before the Romans arrived, long before prehistoric Cro-Magnons and Neanderthals wandered through, year upon year upon year of silence, the beautiful blue water rippling along.

---

173   Nietzsche often asked the people he walked to the site with to sit on the boulder; see Krell and Bates 156.

And you might well find yourself reflecting on the natural processes that went into the creation of this scene: the formation of the planet, the progress and retreat of the glaciers, the depositing of this seemingly permanent boulder as the last glacier retreated. You might well consider how this world of atoms and molecules continually moves and changes and how what looks like permanence really is no such thing, just a moment in the eternal flux that stays stable just a bit longer than do the ephemeral humans who regard it as permanent. You might well start to think, well, *what if* the world-flux runs its course and repeats itself, again and again, eternally, bringing this boulder again and again to this very spot, and bringing you again and again to stand by its side and admire it—what would your reaction be?

And Nietzsche surely affirmed the eternal recurrence at that moment, positioned at that timeless spot, thrilled by his idea, so different from the traditional religious idea that this world is just a temporary vale of tears, a vestibule till we get to enter the true heaven, a place with no change, no character at all. He clearly felt exhilarated to be in touch with this form of timelessness via his embrace of that very moment and with his being the very person he was, destined to have this thought in this very place, and thus able to affirm that he would want to have that thought and be that person over and over into all eternity, "shouting insatiably *da capo*"[174] It's somewhat like the self-affirmation of having lived dangerously and survived.

In an earlier chapter I quoted Krell objecting to the idea that Nietzsche's ideas could fruitfully be connected to specific sites, but I omitted a paragraph which I think will be more relevant now:

---

174   BGE 56 – *da capo* is a musical term, meaning literally "from the head," instructing the musicians to play the same piece again from the beginning.

> The influence of work site on the work cannot be reduced to the site's serving as a reservoir of available metaphors—snowcaps for purity and rigor of thought, the sea for rhythm and fecundity in the writing. The metaphors are rich enough, no doubt; yet their function is highly complex. And the sites themselves—their odors, colors, sounds, silences, virtually everything that goes into the *feel* of them—are inexhaustibly rich. High above the Mediterranean coast or on the shores of Lake Silvaplana it is hard to distinguish the vehicle from the tenor of the metaphor.[175]

Krell seems to be saying two things here. On the one hand, the metaphors that arise from a site are superficial—snowcaps for purity, boulders for endurance through time. And on the other hand, any site will be inexhaustibly rich in possible metaphors, and so Nietzsche on that sparkling morning in August 1881 could well have been prompted by the boulder to muse about the *un*repeatability of moments just as much as their recurrence. As Krell points out too, Nietzsche had been thinking thoughts similar to the eternal recurrence going back at least to his student days.[176]

But I'm still not buying it. Of course, Nietzsche could have had the thought of recurrence elsewhere, and of course he could have had other thoughts sitting by the boulder— and for that matter he surely did, since he surely came back here many times over the decade of summers he spent in Sils. But *pace* Krell, I can quite understand how he had that

---

175   Krell and Bates 6
176   Krell and Bates 5

particular thought at that particular place. And knowing the spot where he had it helps, I think, understand the way in which Nietzsche's thought of eternal recurrence combines as it does both permanence and flux, both boulder and lake, both mountains and sky. For though the boulder and mountains seem permanent, they are caught up in patterns of change just as much as the water and the clouds; though the water and clouds seem the very essence of impermanence, they nevertheless retain the same reality over and over, replaced by different water droplets but still remaining the same lake and the same sky. So while he could certainly have had a lot of different thoughts in that particular spot, it's still easy to understand how he had that particular thought in that particular spot. And even though I first encountered that thought while reading *The Gay Science* in a college library, I definitely feel I understand it better—understand it inside my bones and inside my eyes and all around my skin—while standing by the pyramidal boulder by Lake Silvaplana, "six thousand feet beyond man and time."[177]

THE six of us admire the boulder for a minute or two, then set about looking for the plaque. And we can't find it. We look and we look, and we can't find it. It isn't affixed to the boulder itself, which is what I had expected. It isn't on nearby stones. It isn't hidden in the bushes. It isn't even taped onto the side of the prefabricated outhouse which has been located conveniently nearby.[178]

We look and we look, and the others are getting tired

---

177   EH books.Z.1
178   Yes, really—the price of Nietzsche tourism, I suppose. There's a picnic table there, too. Surely neither were there in 1881, so I guess this is another illustration of how impossible it is to relive Nietzsche's experience.

of looking, but I really don't want to leave without having seen it. After all, I've come almost four thousand miles to see this plaque and I can't imagine ever coming back this way again—not in this particular iteration of the recurrence of the cosmos, at least. But eventually Vicky persuades me to give up. It's quite late, well past lunchtime. The kids will be losing it soon. Plus, it looks like rain. So I give up, a failed Nietzsche freak, doomed to never find the famous plaque over and over again into all eternity.

Before we leave this spot, we find a passerby who will take our picture. Sam hands him his camera. We line up and smile. Our photographer twitches his finger and the moment is preserved eternally. This picture now sits on the dresser in our bedroom. I see it every morning as I get dressed and gather my keys and watch and wallet. There it is—the moment I affirmed the eternal recurrence.

For there we are all together, our size order matching our age order (a moment in time which passed in a year or two after Eli and Miriam shot up to be taller than their siblings). All six of us are hale and happy, and happy *together*, having hiked and having loved the wildflowers and having survived the *holzschlag* together.

That's a moment I'd repeat forever, even though it would bring along with it all the diapers and squabbles and sleepless nights and interrupted conversations and loss of writing time. It's a family that works and I'm part of the team that makes it work. I'd gladly stay standing with them forever by that lake, on that very day, at that very moment.

WE find lunch in the village of Silvaplana at the far end of the lake, then bus home, using free passes provided by the hotel.

And as we spread out in the suite to take our rest, we find that that's not all the hotel is doing for us.

For one thing, the maids appear to have noticed that several of us took apart our *duvets* in the night, using the sheets but not the heavy comforters inside. Rather than robotically reassemble everything, as in our experience hotel maids usually do, the maids at Seraina have folded and stored the heavy comforters and instead re-assembled the *duvets* with a lighter, thinner filling. And they have done this only for those of us who disassembled our *duvets*—Rosie, who likes it thick and heavy, finds her *duvet* still there, evenly smoothed out on just her half of the bed she's sharing with Miriam, whose *duvet* has been altered. Throughout the suite, beds have been made and night tables tidied with acute sensitivity for how they appear to be being used. The maids have even lined up our toiletries for us in the bathroom. We marvel at the Swiss.

But that's not all. As we settle in for feet-up time, the phone rings. I answer. It's someone from the hotel staff. It's a little creepy that they've observed our return, but this, it turns out, is only half of their surveillance.

"It was noticed at breakfast," says the lady on the phone, "that you did not pour yourselves milk." Are we in trouble for not getting our calcium and vitamin D, I wonder? I decide to face the inquisition in a forthright manner.

"The kids like milk," I say, "just not my wife and I." But I have misjudged the lady on the other end.

"Might you like other forms of milk, such as soya milk?"

"Umm, yes, my wife and I would like that very much."

"You will have it tomorrow. Goodbye." And she hangs up.

This, my friends, is my kind of hotel. Nietzsche boasts in *Ecce Homo* that the "old costermonger women of Turin won't relax until they have found their sweetest grapes for me."[179] Surely this was a line they fed every gullible customer, but this particular over-educated one clearly swallowed it whole (pardon the pun). We, I think, are not being similarly self-deluded—they really are taking good care of us.

---

179   EH books.2

Perspectivism & the View from Above

THE NEXT day is July 4th, but the fact that it's Independence Day in the U.S.A. couldn't matter less here in the Engadin region of Switzerland. Such is the difference in our perspectives.[180]

What does matter is that the day breaks clear and beautiful, one of the prettiest days I've ever lived through, the sky cloudless, the pines bathed in sun, and the mountain air crisp in one's lungs. We get that kind of day in Maine too, just not quite so high up. Waking up in the Hotel Seraina at an altitude of 1800 meters plus two flights of stairs, the Professional Travelers are already higher than anywhere in Maine—Mt. Katahdin tops out at 5271 feet and Mt. Blue, after which Farmington's high school is named and which we can see as we go about our daily business, is a mere 3186. And from this already elevated starting point we will be gaining some serious altitude today. Literally the high point of the trip.

We rise, head down for breakfast, and there indeed is a pitcher of soy milk next to the one of regular milk on our table. Vicky and I pour it over a delicious muesli while the

---

180   Would you like to say that at least it's a fact, not a perspective, that in both countries today is the fourth day in the month of July? But there are other calendars people count by, so that's perspectival all over again. But isn't it still the same day, however you label it? No, not even that—at the moment we wake up to July 4th in Sils-Maria, in California it's still July 3.

kids feast on cheese, bread, yogurt and pastry. Then we're out the door to catch the bus to the nearest cable car station.

There are many of these in the Engadine valley, but this is the only one in Sils. The building is all set up for skiing—the flooring has space for melting snow to drain off boots and skis—and is much less crowded than it would be in winter, I imagine. The cable lines carry us straight up the slope of Piz Corvatsch. Looking down, we spot the path we walked on yesterday. After gliding swiftly over the green, flower-strewn lower slopes, the car touches down above the tree line, about halfway up the mountainside at a place called Furtschellas, elevation 2312 meters.

Everyone else in the cable car promptly heads off to the hiking path that starts to the right of the cable car station. We mill around and try to decide which way to go.

Before we left home, Vicky visited a website called "Swiss Panorama *Wanderwege*" (literally "wander ways") which had lots of suggestions for hikes. There was information on altitude covered, degree of difficulty and services available. Among the many she found was one that starts from Furtschellas, heads west (that is, to our right as we exit the cable car) along the ridge, and then descends into the Fex Valley and on to Isola, a little town on the south shore of Lake Sils. The website claimed this particular path features "Excellent view of the Upper Engadin lakes and down to the romantic Fex valley," as well as "Culinary delights at several original restaurants." My wife's always been a sucker for romantic stuff, and I'm always a sucker for culinary delights, so this was our tentative plan coming into the trip. However, on the map of the region supplied by the hotel, there's another path anchored at Furtschellas that's called the *Wasserweg*, literally "the water way." It's called that because it links six small ponds. Unlike the other path, the *Wasserweg* is a loop; taking this route would allow us to return to Furtschellas and ride the cable car back down. It also appears to be shorter than the first and it keeps us at elevation. Like the first path, it also appears to offer food midway at a spot called Rabgiusa which appears, from the map, to be a lovely place to stop and rest.

We dither about this choice for a few minutes, but eventually, on the strength of its ponds and slightly shorter length, the *Wasserweg* wins out and we head off to the left.

Although ponds are what we're looking for, the first moisture we come to, in just a few minutes of walking, is snow. Yes, snow on the fourth of July. Just a patch, mind you, but still, something memorable for us Americans. We rush over to touch it as if it's something we've never seen before, which is silly, of course—we're Mainers. Eli jumps right into the middle of the drift, saying he's going to ski it in his sneakers. Just as he gets down into his tuck, Sam pushes him over. After a brief snowball fight, we move on.

The ponds are indeed spectacular. They remind me a bit of the pond at the top of Tumbledown Mountain, which is near Mt. Blue back home, the highest pond in Maine. Rosie and I once took our summer "playdate" hike up there, and Rosie captured the essence of the spot perfectly when she said, "Good place for a castle." The *Wasserweg* would be a good place for a castle too, though it's quite different. Here we are above timberline, so the vegetation is no longer forest but little Alpine flowers, and then, around each pond, some bright green grass.

At each pond, we find a sign commemorating a series of occasions several years ago when six local children were baptized in these ponds, one per pond, and now the locals call the pond after the name of the child. This strikes us as a beautiful idea.

Our local Jewish group back home ends the Yom Kippur

fast each year at Center Hill in Weld, a spot of incredible beauty—an open ledge with a spectacular view of Webb Lake and a ring of mountains. I wonder what Nietzsche would have thought of the way contemporary religion seeks to connect with the beauty of nature. Religious traditionalists scorn it, but it seems to me a wonderful attempt to blend paganism's reverence for natural beauty with monotheism's transcendence. Nietzsche's main complaint against Christianity is its "otherworldliness," as he calls it.[181] If he were to have found a Christian rite linked to the natural beauty of these high Alpine ponds, I think he would have quite liked it.

Miriam notices that the dates of the baptisms are all in the fall. Presumably this was to avoid the presence of both summer and winter tourists (and in spring the ground would be just like in Maine—quite muddy). The baptisms must have been very moving, what with the whole town hiking up to the ponds in chill, clear autumn air. Everyone would have stood around quietly while a baby cried in the cold water and the bright sun.

Nietzsche writes that mountains have eyes—their lakes are their eyes.[182] I have no idea why he says that—after all, what could the lakes be looking at? I suppose he's thinking of their roundness and their magical, blue reflectivity. It's one of those odd, unguarded passages in Nietzsche's writing which contribute so much to his being beloved by his readers—a bit of childish, poetic individuality that he's not afraid to share in print. I don't think he meant these particular ponds, however; as I've said, I don't think he ever ventured this high up the mountain. Perhaps he was imagining the view from up here. From this height, Lake Sils and Lake Silvaplana do indeed

---

181   Among many other places, see Z I.3 and I.9.
182   GM III.8

look like a pair of deep-set eyes down in the valley below us, with the town of Sils situated in the middle like a nose and Piz Pilaschin serving as the forehead. Of course, it could be one of those reversible drawings, and then it would be the mountain we're standing on that's the forehead. I suppose it depends on one's perspective. The map supplied by the hotel actually takes account of perspectivism by showing the valley twice, once as viewed from the southeast side, where we are now, and once from the northwest side, and the dual perspectives are very helpful in orienting oneself. After all, the more perspectives one tries, the more accurate one's apprehension will be, since there's no single viewpoint that can provide what all the partial views can provide collectively.

We eventually come to Rabgiusa, elevation 2444 meters, where the map indicates that there's food available. However, when we get there all we see is a boarded-up hut. Our first thought is that the restaurant must have closed since the time the map was printed. But then we realize the restaurant is probably only open in the winter, which is the busy season up here—we should have thought of it from that perspective.

Now the issue is: What do we do? It's well past noon and we're hungry. But lunch won't be served here for another four or five months at least. We have only minimal snacks—a handful of peanuts and our last couple of *gianduiotto e grissini* combos from the Milan train station—and more than half our hiking loop still to go.

There commences another dithering session. The kids sometimes get frustrated at the way we make group decisions, what with everyone expressing a view, and with all the going back and forth, some considerations offered and then a moment later withdrawn, all in an attempt to reach consensus. But it is a form of democracy, an attempt to find a balance point amidst the competing considerations, even if in the end, after hearing out the kids' views, Vicky and I wind up making the decision.

Nietzsche's criticisms of democracy are among his most vituperative, for example, when he laments the rise of democracy in the Europe of his own time:

> Today ... only the herd animal receives and dispenses honors in Europe, [and] 'equality of rights' could all too easily be changed into equality in violating rights—I mean, into a common war on all that is rare, strange, privileged, the higher man, the higher soul [etc]....[183]

His understanding of democracy seems to require that there be winners (the formerly disenfranchised) and losers (the unique individuals who are now leveled into an enforced equality), and I suppose that might have made some sense in 19th century Europe, where an established aristocratic class was brought low by successive waves of democratic action. It's less true in 21st century America, where if anything the current trend seems to be towards less equality and towards the development and entrenchment of a distinct aristocratic class. Still, the warning about conformism is surely well-taken, and besides, for Nietzsche (who was not really a noble although he claimed in *Ecce Homo* to be descended from Polish nobility[184]) the following is probably the more important factor in his criticism:

> *Apart.*—Parliamentarianism—that   is, public permission to choose between five basic political opinions—flatters and wins

---

183   BGE 212
184   EH wise.3

the favor of all those who would like to *seem* independent and individual, as if they fought for their opinions. Ultimately, however, it is indifferent whether the herd is commanded to have one opinion or permitted to have five. Whoever deviates from the five public opinions and stands apart will always have the whole herd against him.[185]

Nietzsche's warning may have merit, but I would argue that such figurative violence in democracy is not necessary. As in the Cohen family democracy (when it works), it should be possible in principle for all citizens to be equal participants in discussion and decision-making without their individuality being trammeled.

Ultimately, we decide to press on and complete the loop we started. As we do we begin encountering other hikers, and before long we recognize the people we came up on the cable car with. They had turned right at Furtschellas, while we turned left, but it turns out they were in fact walking the same loop as us, only in the other direction.

Heraclitus, an ancient Greek philosopher whom Nietzsche very much admired for originating the view that the world is nothing but constant flux—which is why "you can't step into the same river twice"[186]—also said, "The way up and the way down are one and the same."[187] These are classic Heraclitean paradoxes. It's one road in a sense, but it's also two different roads depending on your direction of travel. Like the river, its changeable, fluctuating nature is necessary for its static, self-identical nature. Just as the river *has* to be changing in order to stay the same—that is, it has to keep flowing in order to

---

185   GS 174
186   Fragment 91
187   Fragment 60

be a river and not just a long, skinny pond—so too the road has to be two different roads in order to be the same road, because a road connects two places in either direction and so necessarily has two different characters. And this is a classic bit of perspectivism. The path up and the path down are the same path, but they are also very different depending on your perspective, just as July 4th is the same day in Switzerland as in the US and yet not the same day. We are hiking the same path as the people we rode up in the cable car with, only we're hiking up instead of down and so in a sense, it's two different paths.

In this case, though, there is a good reason why they started to the right and not the left, and we soon learn what it is: That's where the highest point on the loop is. They followed the experienced hiker's maxim to do the hardest climbing first, while you're fresh, and gradually descend afterwards. We benighted, dithering amateurs, on the other hand, have spent most of our hike going uphill, and we will wind up enjoying the ease of descent only for a short time at the very end. It's the same path, and yet it's not the same path.

To help ease this unexpectedly strenuous hike and make it more fun for ourselves, the six of us decide to elicit odd looks from the hikers going the other way by greeting them in six different languages: Hello, *Shalom, Bonjour, Buongiorno, Güten Tag*, and *Bun di* (this last is a Romansh greeting we learned only yesterday). Perspectivism can be fun, too.

Nietzsche's Dream *Haus*

CABLE CAR down and bus home, but no time for feet-up—we've got to get there before it closes. We hustle the two hundred meters down the street to the Nietzsche-*haus* for a third time. This time the building is open, and this time we enter. A few steps up, and through the simple wood frame door, and we're in.

I stand still in the entry hall for a long while, noticing everything, taking the time to look at everything, with intent to remember it all. For me this is a shrine.

The first room to the right is where one pays entry, and one can buy books and postcards as well. Durisch, Nietzsche's landlord, was also a merchant of spices and tea, and the layout of the room makes me think the store was probably right here. I picture Nietzsche shambling in from time to time to buy some tea.

In the first room to the left are museum-esque displays of first editions of all his works. I move slowly from book to book, admiring the covers, reading and recalling the paragraphs that have been typed out on little 3 x 5 cards. There's something quaint and 19th century about these displays, in plain white painted wood and glass. No high-tech, push-button displays for this museum—it's as much a monument to the culture of the book as it is a monument to Nietzsche.

There's also an assortment of memorabilia, including photos of him at Weimar in his catatonia.

Haunting the room from a spot high on the wall is his death-mask, a plaster cast model of his face made before burial. It seems ghoulish, but this was a common custom in the days before photography made it much easier to create and store representations of the deceased. Nietzsche's time period is on the cusp of that change—photography was in full swing and we have many photographs of him, but the death-mask custom still continued.

I'm sure those who affixed Nietzsche's death-mask high on the wall of this room had in mind one of his most famous passages:

> Whatever is profound loves masks.... [A] concealed man who instinctively needs speech for silence and for burial in silence and who is inexhaustible in his evasion of communication, *wants* and sees to it that a mask of him roams in his place through the hearts and heads of his friends. And supposing he did not want it, he would still realize some day that in spite of that a mask of him is there—and that this is well. Every profound spirit needs a mask: even more, around every profound spirit a mask is growing continually, owing to the constantly false, namely *shallow*, interpretation of every word, every step, every sign of life he gives.[188]

Sure enough there is his death-mask, hanging high and misunderstood above us, his visitors. Yet the death-mask also makes him present in the room somehow—not just his books, but the man himself.

I am just beginning to commune with Nietzsche when

---

188   BGE 40

my family rushes past, heading for the exit. "We're going shopping down the street," says Vicky, and they're gone. It seems to me that we came all this way just for this, and so I sort of wish they were more into it, but all the same I'm happy to be alone, no one rushing me along, with plenty of time to visit with my friend.

He shambles along beside me towards the back of the house, still on the ground floor, to a room that hosts special temporary exhibits. In the summer of 2008, the display is dedicated to the first English translation of Nietzsche, a multi-volume effort edited by Oscar Levy (also Jewish, like Brandes) and published between 1909 and 1913. A complete first edition set is there, along with panels displaying the history of the project and mini-biographies of the translators.

Among the translators were a couple of women (which one would think would have thrown into question Nietzsche's reputation as a misogynist long ago), including an English woman by the name of Helen Zimmern. Zimmern actually met Nietzsche, first in Bayreuth and later when she spent a couple of summers in Sils-Maria. She had translated Schopenhauer into English and this led Nietzsche to mention her specifically in a letter as a potential English translator for *Twilight of the Idols*.[189] It was not till much later that Levy asked her to help with his project, however, and the works she translated ending up being *Human, All-Too-Human* and *Beyond Good and Evil*. The hotel in Sils-Maria she stayed at when visiting, the Alpenrose, was one of the hotels where Nietzsche often took his lunches. They would meet for meals and also for long walks. There is even a charming account of the two of them going rowing on Lake Sils.

There is nothing more on the first floor after the special display room. A staircase reveals a basement with lavatories

189   Letter to Peter Gast, December 9, 1888 = Middleton #190

and storage in support of the museum, but nothing of interest. So at last the two of us head upstairs.

There is a bedroom on this floor scholars can reserve if they are doing research at the *haus*. It seems not in use just now, and I briefly contemplate trying to sleep there tonight before remembering my family and the wonderful Hotel Seraina. There is also a small garret room, under the eaves, where scholars have sent books they've written about Nietzsche as a sort of homage. I scan the shelves and recognize most of the ones in English. If he knew about this practice, he'd be flattered and gratified, this man who once predicted that someday there would be university chairs devoted entirely to Zarathustra.

A few more steps, and at last—there is Nietzsche's own room, at the back of the house, in the southwest corner.

I stand for a long time at the doorway, looking over the plush velvet rope blocking my entry. I hadn't expected a barrier—but of course the prohibition is not surprising. The room has been refurnished just as it was when he lived there: bed, dresser, washstand, chair, and writing table, all very plain. Oddly, the furniture is in a different configuration than in the picture which appears in Krell and Bates. I find this mildly upsetting, since it means that at least one of these two different configurations must be historically inaccurate. Then I consider that Nietzsche himself probably rearranged the furniture from time to time during what amounted over the years to twenty-one months of living here. In the far corner is the window looking out over the trail that leads up the alpine meadow full of flowers which we hiked yesterday morning.

What would it have been like to live here? Nietzsche would rise to the quiet of a Swiss mountain town. He would write, he would walk, he would write some more. Noontime meal at the Alpenrose, maybe some conversation with Helen

Zimmern, then more walking and writing. The room faces west and would have its best light in the afternoon, though the actual setting of the sun would be hidden by the mountains. After supper, some reading and then to bed. I imagine falling asleep with the window slightly open, the air so quiet and clear and pine-scented, knowing that right outside that window there is a path leading up to an alpine meadow full of flowers.

I leave Nietzsche sitting in his accustomed spot, in the chair by the writing table, and head downstairs to the shop. There I buy a booklet about the house and some postcards which I will eventually tape up on the wall of my office. Some are old photos of Nietzsche himself, of the *haus*, of the pyramidal boulder and of the plaque (but where *is* it?). Someone has printed up a postcard with the words "*und Nietzsche weinte*" ("and Nietzsche wept")—the title of a novel by Irvin Yalom, which has been made into a movie I began watching but found so unfaithful to Nietzsche's actual story, I couldn't stomach it—only the word *weinte* has been crossed out and replaced with *lachte*, turning it into "and Nietzsche laughed." To prove the point, the postcard has a dozen photos of Nietzsche in his prime, all smiling or laughing and looking quite well-dressed (Nietzsche was said to be quite a dandy during his university and early professorship days).

On my way out, I ask the bookstore manager about the famous plaque and point to the postcard picture of it I had just purchased.

"We looked, but couldn't find it," I say.

He is puzzled for a moment and cocks his head to the side. "You looked?"

"Yes, out at Surlej, by the boulder."

Then he understands. "*Ach*, no, it is on Chasté!"

"CHASTÉ!" I say, "It's on Chasté! We were looking in the wrong place! Let's go!" But Vicky and the kids don't catch my excitement. They have shopped and are now deep into feet-up time. But I can't sit still in the hotel room. I'm in Sils-Maria and it's still a beautiful day and I've just learned that the plaque I thought was at the boulder is actually on Chasté and Chasté is just a kilometer or so away. This is our next to last day here, and this is the day, says the Psalm, on which we sing and rejoice.[190] In something of a Nietzschean ecstasy, I head out the door.

NIETZSCHE loved the Chasté peninsula, a long, thin, forested spit intruding into Lake Sils from the east. The name comes from a ruined castle located in the middle of the peninsula. As if he knew Rosie's line ("good place for a castle"), Nietzsche wrote a letter to a friend in 1883, his second summer in Sils-Maria, admitting to the crazy notion of building his own dream *haus* on this spot.[191] The whole peninsula is now public land and might well have been already back in the 19th century. Still, it's a lovely, humanizing anecdote: Nietzsche dreaming of his dream *haus*, a place to get away to from his already-remote Sils-Maria getaway at the Durisch boarding house.

I hustle through the center of Sils-Maria via some back-alley shortcuts—yes, they exist even in such a small place—and out the other side into the open territory between Sils-Maria and Sils-Baselgia. Navigating the back-alley shortcuts

---

190   Psalm CXVIII
191   Letter to Carl von Gersdorff, June 28, 1883 = Middleton #116

gives me great pride—we've only been here a short time, but I've studied the map and am now putting that effort to practical use.

In Nice and Turin, I ventured out alone only on errands to serve my family, but this is my very own quest. Navigating for myself alone, striding at my maximum pace, leaving behind family and town, I come again to a familiar feeling, which I think has always been true for me: When I'm alone, I feel like him. When I'm alone, I'm open to myself and to the world, and I think my philosophical thoughts and my not-so philosophical thoughts, at my own natural and uninterrupted pace. Other people create other centers of concern, other foci. When it's just me, there's an uninterrupted flow between me and the world. I'm noticing everything, open to every view and vista.

I notice, for example, that the Chasté peninsula is heavily wooded and is bumpy with little knolls and dales and ridges, a lot like Maine, actually. I find it a little eerie that he wanted his dream *haus* to be in such a landscape, very similar to the landscape of my actual house.

The path along the southern edge of the peninsula runs alongside a set of posts to which boats are moored. As I walk past I imagine Nietzsche and Helen Zimmern in their 19th century attire, awkwardly getting into a rowboat. I sometimes wonder if there were any romantic sparks between them— being alone together in a rowboat on a beautiful day on Lake Sils would have been a fairly intimate occasion. She was thirty when they first met, only eighteen months younger than he (the same age difference Vicky and I share). Nietzsche describes her in a letter as "A very intelligent woman, very vivacious, an Englishwoman, of course, a Jew!"[192] But as far

192   See Gilman 169, where an anonymous person interviewing Zimmern cites a letter in which Nietzsche describes Zimmern this way. Unfortunately, the date of the letter is not given.

as we know, nothing happened, not even on the rowboat. I think Nietzsche was probably too scarred by the Lou Salomé affair to venture anything with a woman again. For her part, Zimmern gave an interview years later[193] in which she confessed that at the time she hadn't understood much of what he said philosophically. She reported that he was given to quoting *Zarathustra* (three-fourths of which he had completed by that time) at the least opportunity, even though no one else had yet read it, including Zimmern. I can well imagine that Nietzsche said many things in conversation whose meaning one would have to have read all his books to fully understand, and of course her days of translating his works were still many years ahead of her. She attested also that he was gentle and charming, and she vigorously refuted the allegation that Nietzsche's madness had begun early, before his collapse. Elizabeth and the other proto-Nazis often resorted to this claim in an effort to explain away the fact that his published writings were so plainly opposed to their nationalist, anti-Semitic program.

In this interview, Zimmern attests to Nietzsche's having several other female acquaintances in Sils-Maria that summer. There were, for example, the Fynns, a mother and daughter pair (both named Emily) whom Nietzsche actually urged *not* to read his works because he knew their pious English Catholicism would be offended. There was also a young Russian woman named Mansurov, about whom Zimmern tells a remarkable story: Mansurov's mental state had become so troubled that a doctor advised her to go to a sanatorium, but on the day of her scheduled departure she could not be persuaded to leave her hotel room. It was Nietzsche, finally,

---

193 *Living Age,* November 1926. Part of the interview is in Gilman 166-169. If you read German, see the Janz biography, Vol II, 314 ff, for more information about Nietzsche's friendship with Zimmern.

who went upstairs and was able to coax her into the carriage.[194]

Krell and Bates document the fact that other summers brought other women into his Sils-Maria circle—Resa von Schirnhofer, a philosophy student, and Meta von Salis, a Swiss feminist who stayed at the Durisch house a couple of times—according to Krell and Bates, the first women to earn doctorates in Switzerland.[195] Both of these women were happy to converse with Nietzsche and even sought him out when they hit town; they reported him to be gracious and respectful.[196]

All this gives us an impression very different than the usual, accepted one of a Nietzsche sunk deep into isolation and hopelessly misogynistic after the Lou Salomé affair. The man who complained so much in his letters about social isolation, and who did much deliberately to maintain that isolation—who called himself in a couple of letters "the hermit of Sils-Maria"[197]—had a sizable social world there and continued to meet new people throughout his years of nomadic wandering, and among them several women.[198] It's true that after the Lou Salomé affair he never expressed any feelings to a woman again, but the mask he wore included a "courtesy," as he called it, towards the actual women he interacted with. These women found him harmless—"Could this be that same Herr Nietzsche who writes those awful books?"—and they described his way of speaking as charmingly poetic.

---

194   Of all the humanizing anecdotes I've told in this book – his love for chocolate, his plan for a dream haus, etc – this is the one that still blows me away: the gentleness and human-to-human sensitivity it must have taken, and him with his own sanatorium visit just a few years away....

195   Krell and Bates 148; see also 156.

196   Schirnhofer had actually sought Nietzsche out originally as part of her studies, back in April 1884 in Nice, and among other things they attended a bullfight together (!). Salis was the one who purchased the Villa Silberblick, in Weimar, and donated it to Elisabeth as a residence to take care of Nietzsche during his catatonia.

197   See Middleton #126 and #145.

198   Plenty of men too—I'm leaving them out just now.

"I am one thing, my writings are another matter," he writes in his autobiography,[199] and many scholars say we must keep the two apart. But Nietzsche himself said, as we noted earlier, that he profits from a philosopher insofar as the philosopher serves as a life example. It seems that philosophers teach us how to live both from their writings and from their lives. And Nietzsche thus teaches us to live with geniality and gentleness at the same time that he blows everything up intellectually.

I reach the tip of the peninsula at just about the half-hour mark.[200] I have time only to poke at a couple of bushes to try to find the plaque—unsuccessfully—before I must head back so as not to get closed out of dinner (we have learned that at our hotel a dinnertime of 7:00 means they expect you to be in your seats at 6:55). That night I make the Sabbath blessing over a glass of Veltliner, surely a use for it Nietzsche never imagined.

---

199   EH books.1
200   Nietzsche notes in a letter that his walk to Chasté takes him about half an hour too. See Krell & Bates 154-55.

My Children's Land

WE'RE BACK the next morning, all six of us poking around on the Chasté peninsula, and Sam finally finds the plaque. There it is, in plain sight, affixed to a boulder in a little clearing, facing the tip of the peninsula to the west. I was just a few feet away from it yesterday but didn't look in the right direction. Twelve eyes are better than two.

We all gather in the clearing in front of the plaque, in what might as well be the living room of Nietzsche's dream *haus*. We find rocks and logs and clear ground to sit on, Vicky distributes snacks, and then we have our last family philosophical discussion of the trip.

The plaque contains the closing words of the next-to-last section of *Thus Spoke Zarathustra*.[201]   Zarathustra calls it his "drunken song." Here are the words in German:

> *O Mensch! Gieb acht!*
> *Was spricht die tiefe Mitternacht?*
> »Ich schlief, ich schlief –,
> *Aus tiefem Traum bin ich erwacht: –*
> *Die Welt ist tief,*
> *Und tiefer als der Tag gedacht.*
> *Tief ist ihr Weh –,*
> *Lust – tiefer noch als Herzeleid:*
> *Weh spricht: Vergeh!*
> *Doch alle Lust will Ewigkeit –*
> *– will tiefe, tiefe Ewigkeit!*

---

201   Z IV.19.12

And here is Kaufmann's translation (which I actually don't like—I'll explain why below):

> O man, take care!
> What does the deep midnight declare?
> "I was asleep—
> From a deep dream I woke and swear:
> The world is deep,
> Deeper than day had been aware.
> Deep is its woe;
> Joy—deeper yet than agony:
> Woe implores: Go!
> But all joy wants eternity
> —wants deep, wants deep eternity."

Kaufmann manages in his translation to make the English rhyme the way the German does, which I suppose has its value. I usually prefer translations that are closer to the literal, even if the rhyme is lost, and this is how I render it for my family:

> O man, get tough!
> What speaks the deep midnight?
> "I sleep, I sleep
> Out of a deep dream I am awoken.
> The world is deep,
> And deeper yet than the day knows.
> Deep is its woe—,
> Joy—deeper still than heart-pain:
> Woe speaks: Be gone!
> But all joy wants eternity
> —wants deep, deep eternity!"

It's the *gieb acht* in the first line that's the main issue. Kaufmann's "take care" is reasonable enough and of course, it rhymes with "declare" and "swear." It also fits in with contemporary use of the phrase—*achtung* is how Germans warn people of danger. Another reasonable translation would be "Pay attention!", and though it doesn't rhyme, it would be perfectly appropriate in this context, since it's clear Nietzsche wants people to notice and take to heart the deep mystery of life.

But I like "get tough," and here's why. The very same phrase, *gieb acht*, is the phrase that ends the "Why so soft?" passage that we discussed back in Èzé, the one which Nietzsche was inspired to write after witnessing those who preferred the easy road and took the carriage to the top of the hill. There, "get tough" is clearly the meaning. Kaufmann's translation there has "become hard," continuing the trope in the passage contrasting coal and diamond. This again is a reasonable enough translation, but with *gieb acht* having been rendered differently in the two passages, the English reader loses the connection. And there has to be a connection, because the two passages are in the same book, and Nietzsche doesn't choose his words carelessly.

I turn it over to my children. "What does he mean in this poem?" I ask them. "In the earlier passage, the one from Èzé, we understood why he would want people to get tough: Softness, in his view, is what's wrong with modern society— people taking the easy way, the safe way, instead of pushing themselves to create, innovate, achieve, make themselves stronger and by extension, push their culture forward. But here in the plaque passage he's talking about joy—what does that have to do with toughness?"

Eli leads off: "When we're sad, we wish life were over, but

when we're happy we want it to last forever."

"How does that connect to the climbing-the-hill passage?" I ask.

Sam: "Well, rather than avoid difficulties, or explain them away, Nietzsche's telling us to confront them, and that when you do, it will bring growth. Like he did with that three-day migraine you told us about."

I share another passage from *Zarathustra*: "[I]f you have an enemy, do not requite him evil with good … [r]ather, prove that he did you some good."[202]

"In other words," I tell them, "he's saying that when someone does you a wrong, don't thrive *in spite of* what was done to you (and for goodness sake don't turn the other cheek!)—rather, prove that the person did you good despite his evil intentions by utilizing the pain and thus making it a necessary part of your learning and growth. The idea is to grow from your suffering. It's a radical way to think about your life—to see the bad as not merely endurable or overshadowed by the good, but actually necessary for whatever good you do have."

Rosie: "Well, and if you did that, you could really affirm the eternal recurrence, since you'd be able to see why everything that happened to you was necessary."

Miriam: "Yeah, whatever happens to you makes you who you are."

Vicky: "But that makes it sound passive, like it's just happening to you. He seems to me to be saying you have to make an effort to turn the bad into something good—it's not going to happen by itself."

"Remember too," I tell them, "that affirming the eternal recurrence is Nietzsche's definition for a moment of joy. So when you get tough you grow, and growth, in his view, is the

---

202   Z I.19

quintessential moment of joy."[203]

As a group we fall silent. It occurs to me that our trip has come full circle, from *gieb acht* in Èzé to *gieb acht* on the Chasté Peninsula, from the challenge to grow stronger to the recognition of joy at meeting life's challenges. I look around at the kids. They might be reflecting on the discussion or they might just be enjoying the sparkling air and the sun reflected on the lake. Either way, I find myself happy that on this trip they got a chance to meet Nietzsche and he them.

---

203   See A 2.

Epilogue

WHEN DOES A JOURNEY end? It could be checking out of the hotel, or catching the flight home, or finally arriving back home, but I choose to end this philosophical travel memoir here, at the tip of the Chasté peninsula on our last morning in Sils-Maria.

For it's there and then that I realize what this trip was really about. I had seen it as a chance to reflect on the livability of Nietzsche's philosophy, on its relevance and usefulness for life. Visiting his three favorite residences, where he did so much of his writing, provided openings to relate his thought and his life, as well as to relate both of those to my life, so different from his. In Nice I felt deeply drawn to what I've called the Nietzschean notebook life, and I recalled fruitfully some of his most powerful ideas: perspectivism, for example, and the eternal recurrence. In Turin, though, I was more impressed by the value in my life of the social ties he didn't have—marriage, parenthood, and religious tradition—and I found myself pulling away from some of his ideas too, such as his elitism and his rejection of democracy. It would be nice if somehow, here in Sils-Maria, there could be some sort of resolution. Watching my children, post-snack and post-discussion, resume cavorting about the living room of Nietzsche's dream *haus* makes me think I might have found something.

Socrates, on the morning of what he knows will be his death day (according to Plato's fictional imagining of the scene), reports that he has a recurring dream in which he hears a voice telling him, "Socrates, practice and cultivate the arts."[204] Nietzsche alludes to this story when he writes that the ideal philosopher would be "a Socrates who practices music."[205] I take him to mean that this would be someone who combines the kind of rational, logical mind that Socrates is famous for with a soul that is open to the importance of the emotions: "In music the passions enjoy themselves."[206] Such a blend, Nietzsche seems to me to be saying, would result in the best kind of philosopher.[207]

Bringing my children to Nietzsche's land, and discussing his philosophy right there in the living room of his dream *haus*, suggests to me another way of combining lives in a fruitful tension, another blended philosophical ideal—a Nietzsche who has children. The solo notebook-ing life means more, I think, when what you're thinking about includes real relationships[208], especially ones that involve a real and personal

---

204   *Phaedo* 60e, trans Grube.

205   BT 15—Nietzsche actually has this righter than most English translators of Plato, since the Greek word for being engaged with the arts is *mousikos*.

206   BGE 106

207   As just noted, I read "music" in Nietzsche's phrase to be a stand-in for all the arts and indeed for all of our emotions and other non-rational affects. But I admit that he may well have meant it literally, and if so he probably fancied himself as a possible nominee for this role, for he was a talented pianist (especially at improvisation) and, in addition to his philosophical writings composed several musical pieces for piano (including a setting for a poem by Lou Salomé, as I mentioned earlier). When Nietzsche shared his compositions with Wagner, the latter said, "Oh Fritz—you're too good," a backhanded compliment if there ever was one. Later, when Nietzsche heard that Brahms had read *Beyond Good and Evil* with interest, he took it upon himself to send some of his compositions to Brahms. Brahms thanked him for sending them but said no more; this didn't stop Nietzsche from crowing that Brahms had thanked him because he enjoyed his music. To me Nietzsche's piano pieces sound a little bit like Chopin but not as good. They have been recorded, by John Bell Young and others, so you can go hear them for yourself.

208   I don't mean for the word "children" in this paragraph to exclude the child-less – I think it can stand in here for all deep human relationships, the ones that

relationship to the future. And having children provides me with a grounding and basis for real philosophizing that isn't so abstract as to lose touch with life. Nietzsche's philosophical goal throughout his career, through his various changes and intellectual developments, was always to figure out how to affirm life. Although I didn't think of this when I first became a father, I now see that that's what I was really choosing without knowing it. Having children affirms that life is worth living, not merely despite but *because of* all its challenges. It's living dangerously, but with a clear justification.

At the same time, I can't imagine living without that unforgettable voice in my head, pointing things out, looking behind the surface, seeking the deep origins of things, pushing at my assumptions, deepening my insights, raising challenges of his own. Just as one needs two eyes to see in three dimensions, having another mind to bump up against makes one's view of life three-dimensional as well. That's Nietzsche's place in my life, but also, I now see, the place of my wife and children.

"Now I bid thee lose me and find yourselves," says Zarathustra, "and only when you have abandoned me will I return to you."[209] To follow Nietzsche you have to reject Nietzsche. I've walked in his footsteps in Nice and Èzé and Turin and Sils-Maria and the Chasté Peninsula, but I follow him best, I have come to believe, in my children's land:

> Alas, where shall I climb now with my
> longing? From all mountains I look out for
> fatherlands and motherlands. But home I
> found nowhere; a fugitive am I in all cities
> and a departure at all gates. Strange and

Nietzsche, who used the second-person familiar with hardly anyone, mostly missed out on.

209   Z I.22.1

a mockery to me are the men of today to whom my heart recently drew me; and I am driven out of fatherlands and motherlands. Thus I now love only my *children's land*, yet undiscovered, in the farthest sea: for this I bid my sails search and search.

I'm ready to go home.

INDEX

amor dei   38
amor fati   38, 40
Antichrist, The   2, 107
anti-Semitism   15, 16, 21, 123, 125, 143
aristocracy   151, 152, 212
A Winter's Tale   106

Basel   12, 15, 19, 142, 143
Bates, Donald L.   2, 6, 7, 20, 33, 52, 69, 70, 75, 92, 102, 106, 138, 176,
                                  193, 195, 197, 200, 202, 218, 223, 224
Bernina Pass   188, 190, 191
Beyond Good and Evil   2, 46, 61, 109, 138, 140, 153, 217, 231
Birth of Tragedy, The   2, 12
Bizet   26, 71, 187
Borgia   152, 156
Brandes, Georg   20, 145, 217
Burckhardt, Jakob   5, 17, 142, 144, 183, 184

Carmen   26, 71
Chagall, Marc   104-106, 110
Chamberlain   2, 160, 161
Chasté   219-225, 229-232

Danto, Arthur   22
Daybreak   65, 87
Dawn, The   87
Deleuze, Gilles   13
democracy   152, 155, 211-213, 230
Descartes   25
Dionysus   143, 238
Durisch   195, 215, 220, 223

Ecce Homo   2, 8, 17, 47, 54, 87, 101, 143, 163, 164, 177, 205, 212
Eternal recurrence   6, 23, 73, 81, 82, 86-89, 92, 152, 198, 200-204, 228, 230
Èzé   66, 72-74, 79-81, 85-90, 92-95, 97, 101-104, 113, 148, 177, 227, 229,
                                  232

Fino   144, 162
Finzi-Continis   123, 135
Florence   133, 158
Freud   174

Gast, Peter   35, 70, 138, 142, 182, 192, 217
Gauguin   156, 236
Genoa   87, 115, 118, 119, 151
Goethe   26, 118, 144
Good European, The   2, 6, 71, 74, 101, 146

Helprin, Mark   106
Heraclitus   81, 213
Hollingdale, Reginald   2, 22, 87, 236
Human, All-Too-Human   59, 61, 217

Il Trovatore   126
Isis   90, 93, 94, 99

Justine   93, 94, 99

Kal Nidrei   15
Kant   25, 196
Kaufmann, Walter   22, 142
Krell, David Farrell   2, 6, 7, 20, 33, 52, 65, 69, 70, 74-76, 92, 102, 106, 138, 167, 176, 193, 195, 197, 200-202, 218, 223, 224

La Tosca   125
Lutheranism   132

Naumburg   144
Nice   6, 7, 13, 32, 37, 39, 41, 42, 51, 52, 56-63, 66, 67, 70-76, 79, 85, 89, 92-95, 101, 104-106, 109, 110, 115, 118, 120, 126, 132, 151, 155, 159, 161, 177, 179, 193, 221, 223, 230, 232
Nietzsche, Elisabeth   12, 17-22, 82, 144, 145, 223

On the Genealogy of Morals   2, 37, 123-125
Overbeck, Franz   143, 144

perspectivism   9, 43, 44, 46, 47, 49, 50, 51, 61, 152, 211, 214, 230
Pirsig, Robert   100
Plato   153, 231

Rabgiusa   209, 211
Rée, Paul   16, 174-177
Republic   153
ressentiment   35, 37, 38, 40, 139, 238
Rilke   174
Ritschl, Jakob   12
Röcken   11
Rohde, Erwin   161

Salomé, Lou   174, 175, 176, 178, 222, 223, 231, 236
Schopenhauer   10, 24, 166, 217
Sils-Maria   6, 7, 13, 75, 159, 184, 185, 191, 192, 195, 207, 217, 220, 222, 223, 230, 232
Socrates   26, 100, 167, 231

Thus Spoke Zarathustra   2, 21, 73, 74, 99, 177, 178, 225
Tristan und Isolde   35
Turin   2, 5-8, 14, 32, 33, 54, 58, 63, 115-120, 126, 127, 133, 135, 137, 141-144, 146-151, 158-161, 164, 168, 179, 181-184, 193, 205, 221, 230, 232

Venice   6, 14, 149

Wagner   2, 12, 15-18, 27, 28, 35, 78, 107, 143, 174, 231
Will to Power, The   19, 20, 45
will to power   75, 160, 163-167

Zen and the Art of Motorcycle Maintenance   100
Zimmern, Helen   217, 218, 221
Zweig, Stefan   28

ABOUT THE AUTHOR

JONATHAN R. COHEN is a professor of philosophy at the University of Maine Farmington. His first book was *Science, Culture, and Free Spirits: A Study of Nietzsche's Human, All-Too-Human* (Humanity Books, 2010), and his next project concerns Nietzsche's philosophy of music. With their four kids currently scattered up and down the East Coast, he and his wife together maintain a stretch of the Appalachian Trail.

A SELECTION OF OTHER NON-FICTION TITLES BY 8TH HOUSE PUBLISHING

HEIDEGGER'S NIETZSCHE: Being and Becoming by Paul Catanu

Hammering, bombastic, poetic, mystic Nietzsche as seen through the mind of the great ontologist Heidegger. Nietzsche's thought dissected, critiqued, delimited, explored by the author of "Being and Time" one of the most influential modern philosophers of our day, is explored in this insightful new volume, containing never before translated passages from the Nietzschean Nachlass.

By Paul Catanu. 414 pages. ISBN 978-1-926716-02-2. $38.88

THE ENGLISH QABALAH 2nd. Edition, Complete VOLUME

A learned exposition by one of the world's leading Qabalists, this book takes the reader through an exploratory journey through the English Alphabet and the mystic and even subconscious roots of our development of language throughout history.

440 pages | 6 x 9 | Hardcover | ISBN 978-1-926716-27-5

SEVEN SYRIANS - War Accounts from Syrian Refugees by Diego Cupolo

"Seven Syrians" captures the stories and struggles of those caught in the middle of the armed conflict currently ravaging Syria. Framed by Diego Cupolo's unerring eye while touring the region, these photographs and first-hand accounts remind us that it is civilians who suffer the brunt of war's atrocities. In a series of humanizing portraits, Diego Cupolo takes us into the lives of those fortunate enough to have survived the conflict decimating their homeland. Forced to flee their homes and families, these men, women and children, teachers, plumbers, engineers, taxi drivers, brothers and sisters no different than ourselves and our neighbours, tell us in their own words of their struggles, triumphs, pains and fortitude and of the monstrosity of war when all of us the world over, seek the same security and opportunities for our children. Read and listen.

8 x 8. 86 pages, ISBN 978-1-926716-26-8. $18.88

THE MIDAS TOUCH by James Cummins & Cameron W. Reed

"... a journey into the predatory nature of some of the practices and institutions in the financial industry today...."

Authors James Cummins and Cameron W. Reed take us on an exploratory journey into the predatory nature of some of the practices and institutions in the financial industry today. What seems innocently enough as capitalism and greed gone naturally wild in an environment of deregulation, soon appears as deliberate political manoeuvering and close control on an international scale by agents and institutions operating above the law.

5 x 8 . 230 pages. ISBN 978-1-926716-06-0 $23.88

MCGILL LAW JOURNAL - 60 YEARS OF PEOPLE, PROSE AND PUBLICATION

"...a breathtaking picture of a history that was beginning to slowly fade into the past, strengthening the identity of a key part of Canadian society."

The McGill Law Journal is the premiere legal periodical in the history of Canadian scholarship. Since its founding in 1952 by Jacques-Yvan Morin (future leader of the Official Opposition in the National Assembly of Quebec) the Journal has been at the forefront of legal history. It was the first university-based law journal in Canada to be cited by the Supreme Court, and has since been outpaced by no other university journal in the frequency at which the Court has turned to it. And it has always has been run solely by students.

276 pages, Hardcase | ISBN 978-1-926716-25-1| $39.99

TO RUSSIA WITH LOVE by Damian Siqueiros

To Russia with Love" is how a group of Montreal artists and collaborators answer the phobias arising out of Russia. This is their stand against the recent wave of bigotry and violence and the realization of the moral imperative to not remain passive in the face of hatred and injustice.

"...exquisitely detailed...." - Phil Tarney, Artists Corner Gallery, Hollywood, California

"Masterful visual quotations.." - Ivan Savvine, Russian Journalist & Activist

Led by visual artist and photographer Damian Siqueiros, "To Russia with Love" portrays iconic gay and lesbian Russians in all of Siqueiros's usual detail and flare. Along with his collaborators, Mr. Siqueiros is passionate in his belief that fighting hatred with hatred is as nonsensical as trying to extinguish a fire with more fire. There is no condemnation for those perpetrating injustice, instead these portraits serve to remind us of the beauty of love and to validate the couples and the identities of our Russian brothers and sisters in the LGBT community.

THE KNOTTED ROAD by James Cummins

With his 5th book, James Cummins sets the framework for the synthesis humanity seeks between religion and science, empiricism and skepticism, the subjective and objective. A novel paradigm in which these diverging worlds meet, this new epistemology is more than just an interesting read - it could change the way you see everything around you.

248 pgs, 6 x 9. ISBN 978-0-9809108-4-1. $24.88

Lightning Source UK Ltd.
Milton Keynes UK
UKHW041554051118
331796UK00001B/288/P